THE MAXIMALIST PHOTOGRAPHER

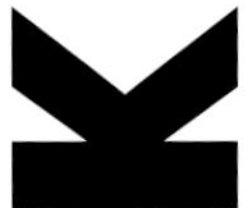

First published in Great Britain in 2026 by Laurence King, an imprint of The Orion Publishing Group Ltd, Carmelite House, 50 Victoria Embankment, London EC4Y 0DZ

An Hachette UK Company

The authorised representative in the EEA is Hachette Ireland, 8 Castlecourt Centre, Castleknock Road, Castleknock, Dublin 15, D15 XTP3 , Republic of Ireland (email: info@hbgi.ie)

10 9 8 7 6 5 4 3 2 1

A CIP catalogue record for this book is available from the British Library.

ISBN (Paperback) 978 1 39963 658 2
ISBN (eBook) 978 1 39963 659 9

Commissioning Editor: Laura Paton
Art Director: Liam Relph
Senior Designer: Hannah Beatrice Owens
Designer: Irina Selaru
Picture Researcher: Penelope Bowden – Proudfoot Pictures
Production Manager: Amy Cadman

Origination by F1 Colour
Printed by C&C Offset Printing Company Ltd., China

Typeface: Freight Text Pro
Text paper: 157gsm Golden Sun matt art FSC
Case: 5/0 (CMYK + PMS 923 C) on 350gsm 1/s artboard FSC

Front cover: *Ahmed Legs*, from the *Legs* series, Hassan Hajjaj, 2022/1443
Back cover: *Trackwork*, Antony Zacharias, 2023

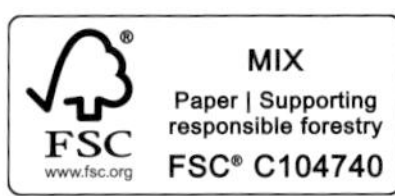

www.laurenceking.com
www.orionbooks.co.uk

THE MAXIMALIST PHOTOGRAPHER

50 TECHNIQUES FOR CAPTURING BEAUTY IN EXCESS

ANTONY ZACHARIAS

LAURENCE KING

Composition

Light, Colour and Contrast

CONTENTS

Creative Techniques

Storytelling

INTRODUCTION

Photography is an art of choice that is shaped by our vision and intent: what we as the photographer choose to include or leave out of a picture, and how we arrange the subject or scene within the frame.

A photograph usually tells a story, evokes emotion or conveys a narrative, and this is often easier to achieve by simplifying the content for the viewer. Maximalist photography, however, turns this on its head. Instead of encouraging restraint, it is about embracing excess and complexity, and including abundant details to offer an alternative and arguably more compelling way to tell your visual stories.

Maximalism in photography thrives on excess to create layered, intricate compositions that require – and also reward – exploration. It is a style that offers an overwhelming sensory experience for the viewer, where each photograph is filled with detail, texture, colour and narrative, all simultaneously competing for attention.

Whether you're shooting bustling street scenes, highly stylized portraits or intricate still-life arrangements, the principles of maximalism can help you create images that are energetic and unforgettable. It is about seeing photography not just as a means of capturing reality, but as a way of creating rich, intricate frames that are both dynamic and engaging.

However, while this approach rejects the notion that a photograph must be simple to be impactful, maximalism is not purely about cramming as much as possible into a photograph. There is a skill to its execution – a careful balance between complexity and intention. It is not just about filling the frame for the sake of it, rather layering elements in a harmonious and logical way.

This book is designed as a creative companion for photographers looking to master the art of maximalism in their images. Over the pages that follow, you will explore a range of techniques that will help you challenge the conventional confines of what is considered 'too much', to build richer and more vibrant photographs. Starting with composition – the keystone of all photography – you will learn how to create a compelling maximalist photograph. You will see how light, colour and contrast all influence the subject or scene, and discover creative ideas and techniques that can lead to a well-crafted and immersive visual experience. Finally, you will explore ways to address the story behind an image; to guide the narrative and evoke an array of emotions in the audience through a maximalist frame.

As you work through these techniques, allow yourself to experiment freely. Break traditional rules, embrace bold choices and develop your own maximalist style. Whether you are drawn to high-energy compositions, an extravagant use of colour or detailed storytelling, this book will provide you with the tools to craft photographs that are as complex, immersive and intriguing as the world around you.

WHAT IS MAXIMALISM?

Maximalism is more than a visual style: it is a way of thinking, seeing and creating. It rejects the minimalist approach of simplicity and restraint to achieve clarity, instead reveling in abundance, intricacy and detail. Whether in art, design, fashion, literature, music or even lifestyle choices, maximalism thrives on the idea that 'more is more' and that bold, elaborate, vibrant layers can create a deeper and more immersive experience for the audience.

Although the term 'maximalism' is relatively modern, the aesthetic has existed for centuries, appearing in various forms across different eras and cultures. Historically, it can be traced back to movements such as Baroque and Rococo art, where elaborate ornamentation, intricate patterns and luxurious materials were used to create dramatic and emotionally powerful works. In the 19th century, the Victorians embraced a maximalist approach in their interior design, with richly decorated rooms, patterned wallpapers and an abundance of furniture and decorative objects.

Recently, there has been a resurgence of maximalism. It has resurfaced in various forms, from the bold patterns of postmodern architecture to the eclectic mix of styles in contemporary fashion and interior design. Today, maximalism continues to evolve, manifesting in everything from digital art and music, to branding and social media, and while it varies among different disciplines, at its heart lies a universal approach that embraces excess.

In photography, maximalism is about including more than may be initially needed: more layers, more texture, more contrast, more narrative. It draws the viewer into the frame and invites them to explore it slowly, rather than absorbing it in a single glance; it rewards time and close attention. Maximalism is a style that welcomes curiosity, encouraging the viewer to drift through the photograph, discovering moments, gestures, contrasts, symbols and meaning hidden within the layers of the frame.

Maximalism is not just about quantity, though. It is a deliberate and artistic arrangement of elements. A maximalist photograph contains carefully curated complexity; it is a frame filled with purpose, where every inclusion is considered and every detail contributes to the overall composition. The layers of chaos are apparent on the surface, yet underneath them lies a complex framework of thought and intent.

Importantly, maximalist photography isn't confined to any one genre or subject. It can be found across diverse subjects and scenes: from chaotic streets in urban photographs, to the saturated patterns of a highly stylized fashion shoot, or the intimate layers found in the home. A maximalist image might contain multiple elements or objects, or it may feature just a few that are captured with such depth, repetition or variation that it feels intricate and saturated. What matters is not the number of elements in the frame, but how they relate to one another and how they interact to create a complex visual experience.

Maximalist photography often draws strength from compositional techniques such as reflections, patterns, density and layering, which can be used to build tension, create harmony or evoke surprise in the viewer. Colour, in particular, can play an important role in maximalism. Bold, vibrant palettes or highly saturated hues are often used to heighten the intensity of an image, but maximalist colour can also be about subtle relationships – shifts in tone or hues, or the layering of colours that deepen the scene without overwhelming it. A maximalist image can be loud or surprisingly muted, or even without any colour at all, but in all cases colour is used not just decoratively, but structurally. It becomes a tool that helps create contrast and depth, and evoke emotion.

Narrative, too, is central to the maximalist approach. The photograph isn't just a fleeting moment – it contains a story with multiple competing or overlapping narratives. These stories don't have to be literal. They can be felt through gesture, composition, spacing or even through the chaotic visual overload itself. In this way, the viewer becomes an active participant in finding meaning within the fragments, details and other aspects in the frame.

Ultimately, though, maximalism is about bold storytelling and the celebration of richness, detail and complexity. Whether in art, design or daily life, maximalism reminds us that sometimes, more really is more.

COMPOSITION

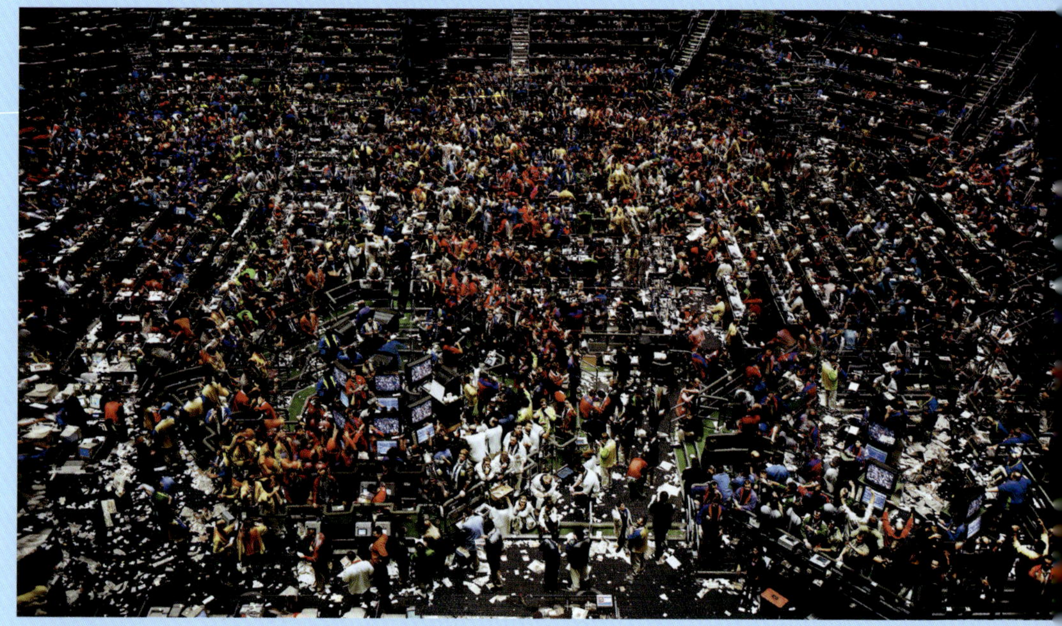

Chicago Board of Trade II, Andreas Gursky, 1999

EXCESS

FIND HARMONY IN CHAOS

Maximalist photography thrives on the edge of chaos, with every detail in the frame competing for attention. However, it is not about capturing or creating disorder: it's about finding a balance in the abundance.

Incorporating excess into a photograph requires you to abandon any thoughts of simplifying the scene. Every corner of the frame should be filled with texture, colour, pattern, shadow and light, so rather than possessing a single isolated subject, the frame becomes a network of interconnected parts. Intent is important, as without careful thought the photograph can easily lose its effect and become overwhelming. When every element contributes to the story, the resulting composition will feel dense, with a deliberate sense of purpose.

Andreas Gursky's *Chicago Board of Trade II* is all about excess. The image captures a crowded scene that is full of colour and detail. At first, it feels chaotic, but on closer inspection there is an intricate rhythm: the repetition of people and scattered papers creates a sense of harmony where every element contributes to the larger story of economic frenzy. The image transforms overwhelming abundance into something structured and dynamic, as it offers the viewer a chance to immerse themselves in the energy and activity of the financial trading floor.[1]

When used thoughtfully, excess amplifies emotions. A photograph full of content naturally immerses the viewer, inviting exploration and engagement. When every element in the frame contributes to the mood or narrative, abundance becomes a strength rather than a distraction. Excess can overwhelm the senses, but in doing so, it mirrors the way we often experience real life.[2]

One of the challenges when working with excess is ensuring that the photograph remains cohesive. This is where composition becomes critical. Techniques such as leading lines, framing or layering can help guide the viewer through the image, suggesting a sense of order without losing the spontaneity and vibrancy of the moment.[3] [4]

When composing an image, it can often be difficult to let go of the fear of 'too much'. Start by seeking environments that are naturally busy and cluttered, such as markets, festivals or dense urban spaces. Then, instead of narrowing your focus of attention, challenge yourself to include more. Pay attention to how the elements interact and the overall flow of the image. Does the abundance enhance the mood or message? Ultimately, excess should help elevate the scene into one that feels alive with detail and invites the viewer to explore further.

[1] *See* Beauty in Chaos pp. 86–9
[2] *See* The Everyday pp. 124–6
[3] *See* Leading Lines pp. 18–19
[4] *See* Framing pp. 66–7

VISUAL INTENSITY

FILL THE FRAME WITH PURPOSE

A maximalist photograph will naturally contain a wealth of detail, but the frame shouldn't be filled with elements that don't logically fit or work together. Filling the frame with purpose means using the available space to include a multitude of elements that help to tell a richer, more immersive story. Doing so will result in a compelling image where the viewer is drawn into the dense, layered scene.[1]

It is vital to ensure that everything included in the frame serves a clear function, whether that's guiding the viewer, setting the mood, reinforcing emotion or revealing essential details about the scene.

The image shown here demonstrates how an urban scene can be filled with meaningful content. On a snowy day in Manhattan, taxis dominate the foreground, while a pedestrian crosses the street, framed by the cars. The towering buildings rise on either side, stretching the depth of the frame. Although the scene is packed with visual information, there's a sense that each part of the image has been included intentionally. The city architecture recedes into the background, adding context without becoming mere clutter. Even the snowfall contributes to the atmosphere, emphasizing the chilly conditions and the hurried pace of city life.

A key consideration is to pay attention to how you position your main subject(s) in relation to other elements in the frame. Here, the taxis are prominent, but they don't overshadow the person or the buildings. The street-level viewpoint gives the feeling of being in the midst of the action,[2] which creates a sense of immersion that's central to the idea of maximalism. Rather than standing back and observing, the viewer is invited into the scene, surrounded by detail on all sides. You also need to be mindful of what happens at the edges and corners. If any part of the composition feels unfinished or irrelevant, it risks drawing the viewer's attention away from the core story.

It is also important to look at the relationship between the elements. Each object, texture or colour should contribute to the balance and rhythm of the composition. Visual weight plays a significant role here, with stronger elements anchoring the scene and smaller details helping to create connections that unify and explain the image. Careful placement will ensure that the abundance of information remains engaging rather than overwhelming. The challenge lies in leading the viewer's eye on a deliberate visual journey, where every element is essential to the story you are telling.[3]

[1] *See* Multiple Narratives pp. 110–11
[2] *See* Exaggerated Perspectives pp. 30–1
[3] See Organized Chaos pp. 16–17

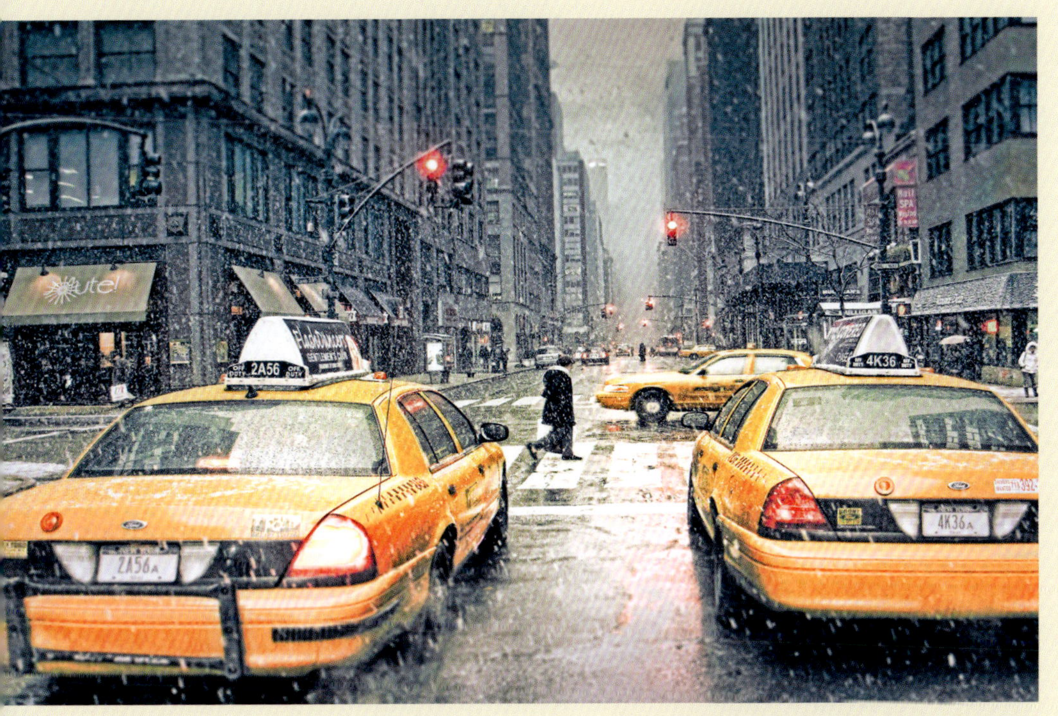

West Side Winter, NYC, Antony Zacharias, 2007

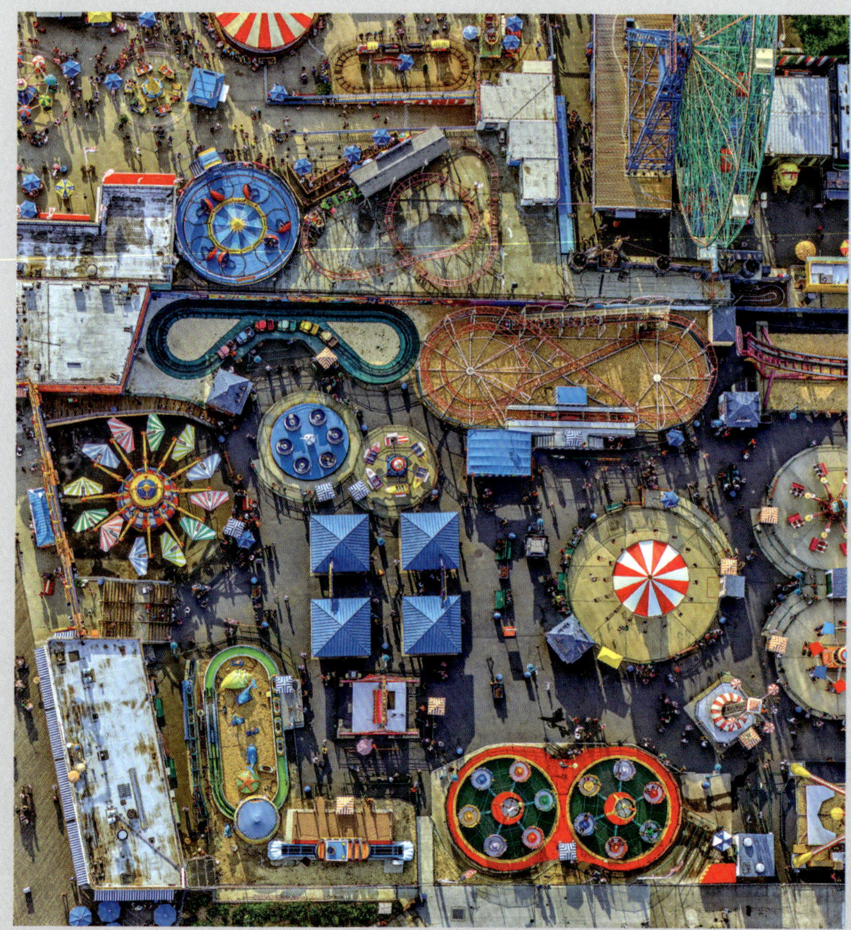

Coney Island 2, Jeffrey Milstein, 2017

ORGANIZED CHAOS

USE STRUCTURE TO BALANCE DISORDER

Jeffrey Milstein's image, *Coney Island 2*, reveals the amusement park from above: the rides, tents and other attractions fill the frame with a chaotic mixture of shapes and colours. The eye naturally darts from one area or object to another, as each vies for attention. Yet, despite the abundance in the scene, there is a surprising sense of harmony, as natural lines are formed from the pathways, which help guide us around the image. The way the structure and chaos work together is what makes the image so compelling.[1]

Organized chaos is about creating a sense of narrative through visual overload. Although all of the objects or elements might seem uncoordinated or haphazard at first glance, they work together to form a unified and meaningful whole. They each serve a purpose within the broader story you are telling, without distracting from the main focus.

This is a powerful way to take a scene that is overflowing with details and guide the viewer to see it as a cohesive image, even when this is not immediately obvious. It is achieved through the careful placement of elements – colours, textures, shapes and subjects – throughout the frame. These may not be obvious when looking at smaller sections of the image, but they emerge as the picture is viewed as a whole. At the heart of this technique is the idea that even seemingly overwhelming compositions possess an underlying structure that unites the elements to form a meaningful visual experience.

It is vital that the composition feels vibrant rather than cluttered, as this is what will encourage the viewer to explore further without feeling overwhelmed or intimidated. A good way to do this is to highlight any patterns and rhythms that structure a scene. Colour, shape and geometry will also help bring order to a busy scene, each contributing to the composition's overall balance.

Lighting (and, by extension, shadows) can further enhance or subdue the sense of chaos. In a bright daylight setting, every colour and shape will appear vibrant, making the scene feel dynamic and full of life. Conversely, cloudy skies will soften the light, reducing contrast and muting tones, which can bring a sense of calm or subtlety to even the most complex composition.

A strong vantage point is another way to help organize the chaos within a scene. In this image, the aerial perspective reveals an intricate design that is impossible to see from eye level. Elevation provides a natural way to frame the scene, allowing the viewer to appreciate how each element interacts with the others.

[1] *See* Exaggerated Perspectives pp. 30–1

LEADING LINES

GUIDE THE EYE THROUGH COMPLEXITY

Leading lines are a fundamental tool in photographic composition, helping guide the viewer's eye through a scene, towards specific areas. In an image that is full of detail, texture and complex visual information, the strategic use of leading lines becomes even more important. Instead of letting the abundance of shapes, tones and textures overwhelm the viewer, lines can be used to create a sense of direction and flow through the image. These compositional lines – whether literal or implied – can be used to help navigate the visual complexity.

Lines don't have to be straight or obvious. They can curve, intersect, zigzag or appear fragmented, and they'll still work to structure the image and connect its components. They do not have to always lead to a single subject either. In maximalism, the goal is often to draw attention to a broader composition or suggest a pathway through layers of meaning.

In this haunting seascape, leading lines play a subtle but powerful role in guiding the viewer through the layered drama of the composition. The sweeping curve of the shoreline starts in the foreground and gently arcs towards the towering sea stacks in the distance, drawing the eye across the full depth of the scene, while the repeating lines of water, left by retreating waves, enhance the sense of movement and rhythm. These elements work together to create a maximalist image that is both vast and immersive, with the leading lines providing structure and flow through the complexity.

In some images, the lines themselves can be the subject, but they can also be combined with other compositional tools to help establish order and balance in the visual chaos. A diagonal pathway may lead to a cluster of focal points, for example, while intersecting lines might form a grid that organizes the image into zones of interest. Repetitive lines can help create a sense of rhythm, adding another layer to an image.

Perspective plays an important role, too. Your camera angle and position will determine where lines are placed within the frame, while your choice of focal length will affect how those lines are portrayed in the frame. A wide-angle lens, for example, can be used to exaggerate space and depth, drawing the viewer into your scene.[1]

It is important to avoid the overly rigid use of leading lines. Lines should feel natural and integrated, not forced or dominant. In a scene that is already filled with visual interest, they should enhance how the viewer's eye travels through your photograph.

[1] *See* Exaggerated Perspectives pp. 30–1

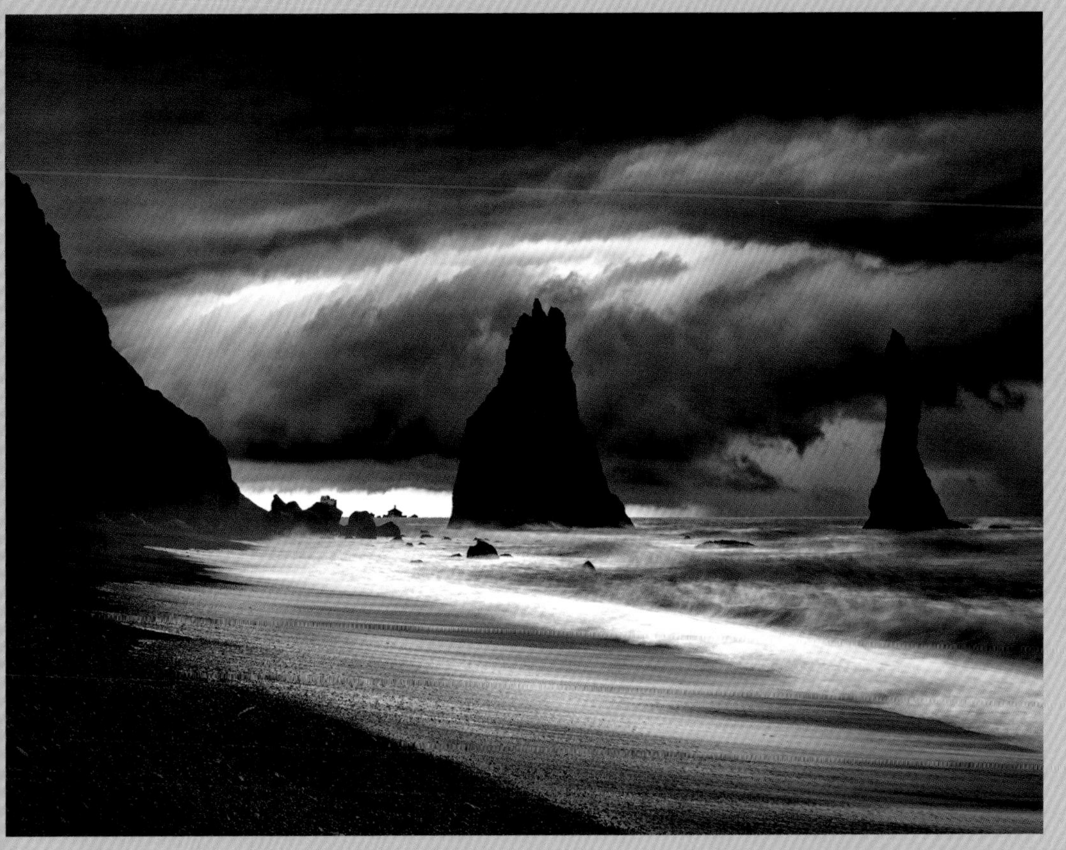

Reynisfjara, Antony Zacharias, 2011

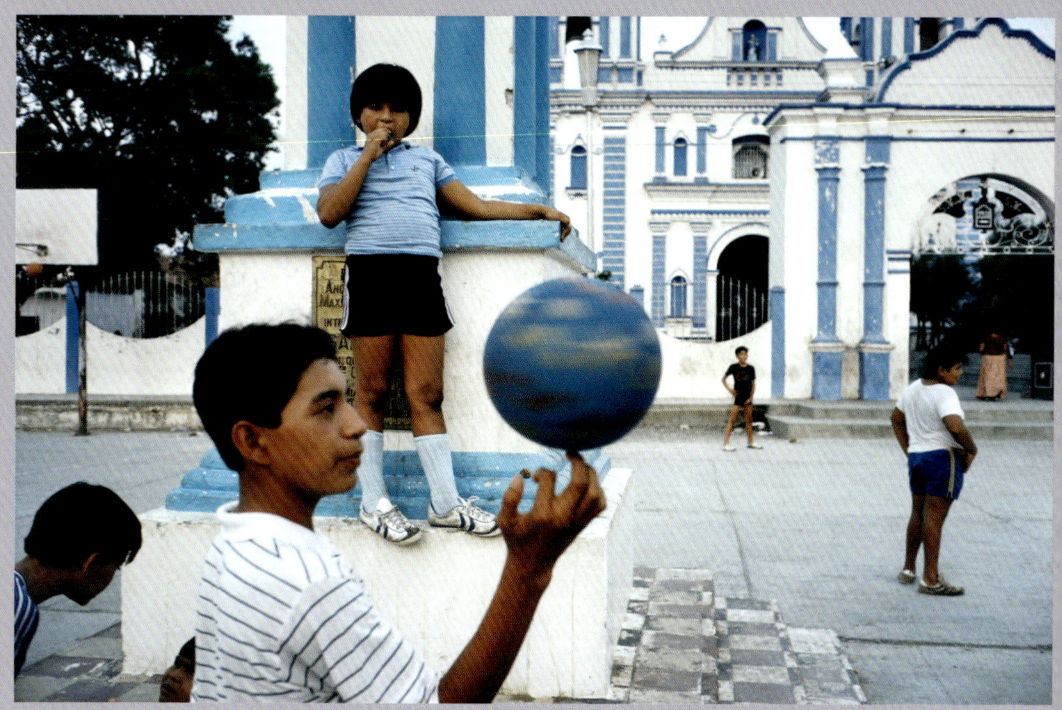

Tehauntepec, Mexico, Alex Webb, 1985

MULTIPLE FOCAL POINTS

GO BEYOND A SINGLE SUBJECT

Creating images with more than one focal point invites the viewer to actively explore the frame, discovering different stories that are unfolding simultaneously. The result can be a photograph that feels exciting, as a variety of connections, details and layers of meaning are uncovered. When captured in a considered way, such images can be incredibly compelling.

However, there is a fine line between visual complexity, chaos and overwhelming confusion. An excess of random objects or unrelated scenes is likely to lead the viewer feeling uncertain and bewildered as they search for a meaning or understanding in your image. It is crucial that each visual element maintains its own strength while also contributing to the overall narrative. As the viewer wanders through the frame, each focal point should not only provide a point of interest but also form part of a larger story.

Alex Webb puts this maximalist approach into practice in the image presented here. It captures an everyday scene full of life and activity where each individual is engaged in their own actions. In the foreground, a boy spins a ball on his finger, which grabs our attention, but the child leaning casually against a pillar gazing back at us, and other figures in the frame, add layers of interest and narrative possibilities. The combination of architectural details and an engaging colour scheme enhances the sense of place and the visual complexity of the image. Each individual focal point presents a different story, yet together they form part of a much larger scene.

To effectively capture multiple focal points, it is important to carefully consider perspective, depth of field and framing.[1] A broader view can allow more elements and different layers to be included in the image, and a wide-angle focal length can help in this regard.[2] A large depth of field will ensure clarity throughout the image, from the foreground through to the background, which can be achieved by using a small aperture setting. This will also help ensure that each focal point appears with equal sharpness and weight in the frame.[3]

Positioning each focal point at a different distance within the frame forms layers that create a sense of dimension and intrigue. Layers also provide a natural pathway through the composition that helps establish a sense of narrative. Colours, contrasts and compositional lines can subtly guide the viewer's eye between these points, ensuring a sense of coherence amid an abundance of detail.[4]

[1] *See* Framing pp. 66–7
[2] *See* Exaggerated Perspectives pp. 30–1
[3] *See* Multiple Narratives pp. 110–11
[4] *See* Leading Lines pp. 18–19

OVERLAP

BUILD CONNECTIONS BY LAYERING ELEMENTS

Overlapping the subjects in a visually rich scene will add depth and complexity to a photograph, and can help create a feeling of cohesive abundance. By stacking subjects, layering visual elements and partially revealing others, you can transform a scene into one that is seemingly more structured and intentional.

Allowing elements to intersect and interact within the frame can establish relationships between them that not only help guide the viewer's eye but contribute to the narrative of the image. It creates a subtle feeling of rhythm that helps the viewer flow through the scene from one section to another, rather than jumping around the frame from one area to the next.[1]

Overlaps naturally mirror the way we perceive the world. Our surroundings are rarely neatly organized or viewed in isolation – they are layered with objects and subjects that are constantly blending into one another. Capturing this reality invites the viewer into the scene and makes them feel as if they are immersed in it.

The image here captures part of London's dense metropolitan skyline, with layers of architectural styles that overlap to create a varied visual narrative. The shorter, older brick buildings in the foreground contrast with towering, modern glass skyscrapers.[2] These facades of city buildings and their precise alignment of windows, bricks and glass panels creates subtle visual rhythms that tie the image together.

To embrace overlap effectively, it must be approached with intent; the overlaps should be a deliberate choice that enhances the composition. Pay careful attention to alignment, tonal contrast and subject placement to ensure that overlapping elements contribute to the image's balance and clarity rather than detract from it. Look for elements that intersect in a way that feels natural and not staged.

Your vantage point, framing and distance can all affect how the overlapped elements are perceived.[3][4] Shooting from a slightly angled position – rather than straight on – can visually compress the depth of the scene causing planes to overlap more dramatically, while elevated or lowered viewpoints can manipulate the order and relationship of the visual elements. At the same time, a longer focal length can flatten a scene, enhancing the sense of layering by reducing visible space and depth. This effect is demonstrated in this image, which was taken with a 200mm telephoto lens to compress the layers of architecture.

[1] *See* Multiple Focal Points pp. 20–1
[2] *See* Juxtaposition pp. 130–1
[3] *See* Framing pp. 66–7
[4] *See* Exaggerated Perspectives pp. 30–1

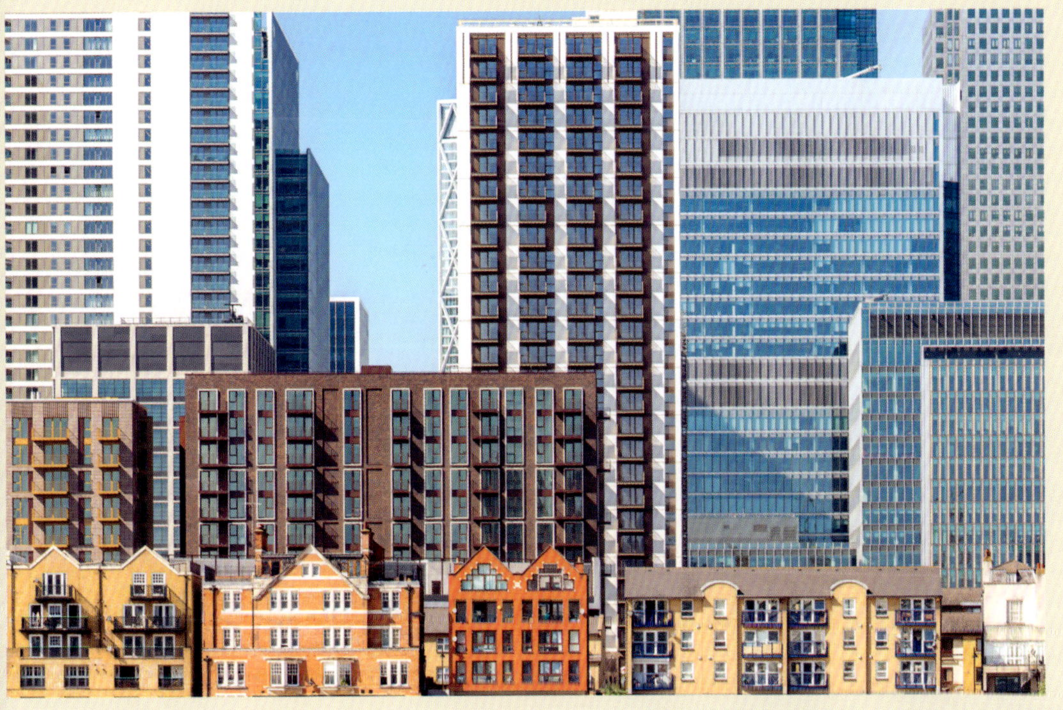

Docklands, London, Antony Zacharias, 2018

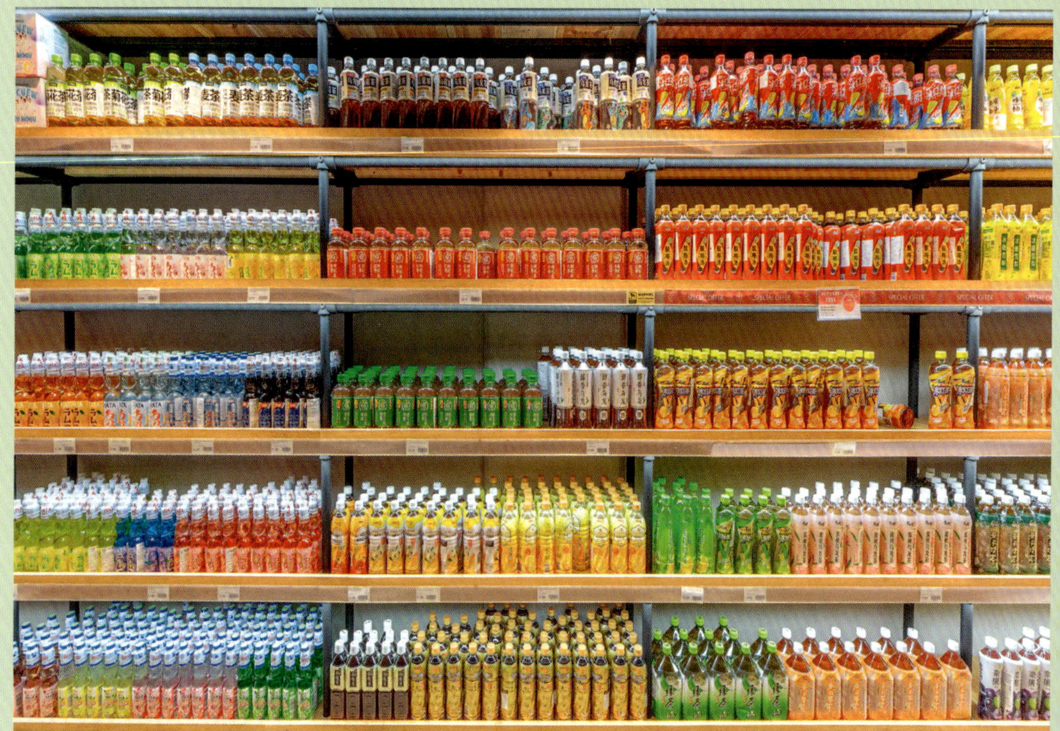

Lined Up, Antony Zacharias, 2022

PATTERNS

USE REPETITION TO ADD RHYTHM AND MOVEMENT

Incorporating patterns in a maximalist composition is a powerful way to add rhythm, structure and complexity. Repetition can introduce a feeling of movement, which can provide an added dimension that helps create a visually rich experience for a viewer.

The key to integrating patterns effectively lies in the way they interact with the other elements in the frame. Deciding how prominent you want the pattern to appear is an important consideration: it can serve as a passive backdrop or a more active part of the composition. Both have the power to enhance the visual impact, but in very different ways.

Uniform patterns capitalize on the hypnotic appeal of repetition. When an element continues through the frame, it can provide a sense of order and stability that can help anchor an otherwise overwhelming scene. The repetitive elements add to the complexity of the image, but also play an important role in guiding the viewer and giving them a momentary break from the details in the composition.

In *Lined Up* – an image of neatly arranged bottles in a store – each row appears sorted by colour or brand. Initially, it looks like a grid of repeated shapes, but there are subtle shifts in tones and colours. In a maximalist style, the entire wall of bottles fills the frame, presenting a repetition that somehow feels orderly rather than overwhelming. The viewer is compelled to scan from one row to the next, noticing how each hue transitions to the next and the shapes align. Despite the abundance of details, the uniform pattern creates a calming and methodical sense of rhythm throughout. One of the advantages of a uniform pattern lies in how it can help the viewer navigate an image. Each repeating pattern presents a familiarity that makes a scene feel coherent, despite the potential for a visual overload.

Compositionally, you can approach a pattern in a variety of ways. A straightforward head-on view will showcase any repetition clearly, whereas an angled view can add a sense of depth as repeating forms recede into the background. Tilting the camera can often introduce a dynamic effect without diminishing the strength of the pattern.[1]

[1] *See* Organized Chaos pp. 16–17

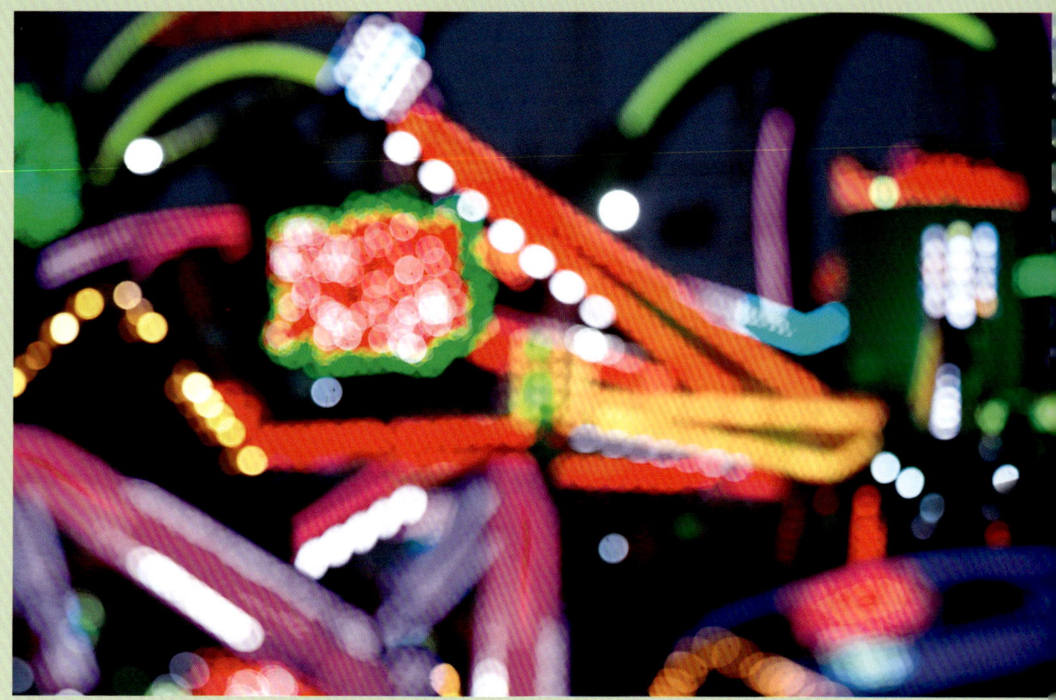

Afterglow, Antony Zacharias, 2018

PATTERNS

Irregular patterns celebrate the beauty of unpredictability. Shifts in shape, colour or position can exude an energy and sense of movement that draws the viewer's eye.[2] In *Afterglow*, the neon blur of the carnival rides was captured at night. Deliberately defocusing the lens resulted in vivid streaks of vibrant colours that seem to spin through the frame. Despite their lack of uniformity, the overlapping lights create chaotic patterns that become the subject, seemingly alive with energy. As no two elements are exactly the same, the image doesn't have the rigid structure of the previous photograph and there isn't an obvious path for the viewer to follow through the scene. However, the similarity of shapes and colours hints at a 'pattern within a pattern', which keeps the composition lively and invites curiosity; it is for the viewer to create their own sense of order.

Capturing irregular patterns requires careful consideration when it comes to balancing the abundance of shapes or colours without them appearing too random and chaotic. One technique is to identify a focal point that appears naturally from the pattern, and position it strategically in the frame. This can help to give structure to the image and provide a 'base' from which the viewer can explore the photograph.

Think about how colour plays a role in pattern-based maximalist compositions. Bright, vivid hues can amplify the sense of a pattern or make it appear more prominent[3], while muted tones can help patterns blend more harmoniously, creating a sense of depth without overpowering the frame.[4]

Contrast and variation within patterns will also contribute to how captivating the audience finds the image. Combining strong geometric shapes with other more organic elements often creates a dynamic composition that feels more interesting and compelling.[5]

Ultimately, patterns can serve as structural and design elements that can transform a scene, with repetition and variation both contributing to the energy of an image. Thoughtful layering and integration can result in images that celebrate excess, while still maintaining a feeling of cohesion.[6]

[2] *See* Abstracts pp. 82–3
[3] *See* Explosive Colour pp. 46–7
[4] *See* Emotive Colour pp. 48–9
[5] *See* Shape and Geometry pp. 78–9
[6] *See* Repetition pp. 70–1

SYMMETRY

BALANCE COMPLEXITY WITH VISUAL ANCHORS

Symmetry is a cornerstone for organizing visual abundance, helping to transform overwhelming details into something more considered and orderly, and enabling the eye to move more fluidly through the scene. This symmetry doesn't need to be perfect, though – often it emerges through near-repetition, mirrored forms or a thoughtful distribution of visual weight.[1]

Here, the impact of the brutalist architecture is heightened by the centred composition, with a strong central axis running vertically through the middle of the frame. This helps to highlight the strong converging lines and vertical columns that draw the eye towards the central doors. The combination of symmetry and maximalism gives a sense of balance to the geometric design of lines and shapes.[2]

In this example, symmetry is not just a compositional feature – it helps to emphasize the visual density and scale of the architectural forms. The repeating patterns, sharp angles and clean lines create a visual rhythm that feels both meditative and dynamic. While the structure is complex, symmetry simplifies the viewing process, allowing the eye to explore detail while never losing orientation.

Incorporating symmetry into your maximalist photography starts with observation. Seek out environments that are rich in detail and identify strong visual anchors such as doorways, arches or central figures that can serve as a focal point. These anchors can help organize the abundance of textures, patterns, shapes and light within the frame.[3]

To refine your symmetrical images, experiment with framing to create immersive experiences that transform complexity into visual order.[4] Leading lines can help to guide the eye towards the centre of the frame to enhance the balance and flow of the composition.[5] Different angles and camera positions can also help uncover unique perspectives that enhance the symmetry. However, small misalignments or inconsistencies in patterns can easily disrupt the balance, so consider using a tripod and the grid overlay function on your camera for precise framing. Additionally, take time to review the frame carefully, checking for anything that might break the symmetry.

Post-processing also has a part to play in fine tuning the balance of an image, by correcting minor misalignments or amplifying the visual appeal of repeating patterns.[6] However, restraint is key here – symmetry should support the complexity of the image and amplify the structure that is already present in the frame, rather than imposing an artificial perfection.

[1] *See* Reflections pp. 68–9
[2] *See* Shape and Geometry pp. 78–9
[3] *See* Patterns pp. 25–8
[4] *See* Framing pp. 66–7
[5] *See* Leading Lines pp. 18–19
[6] *See* Repetition pp. 70–1

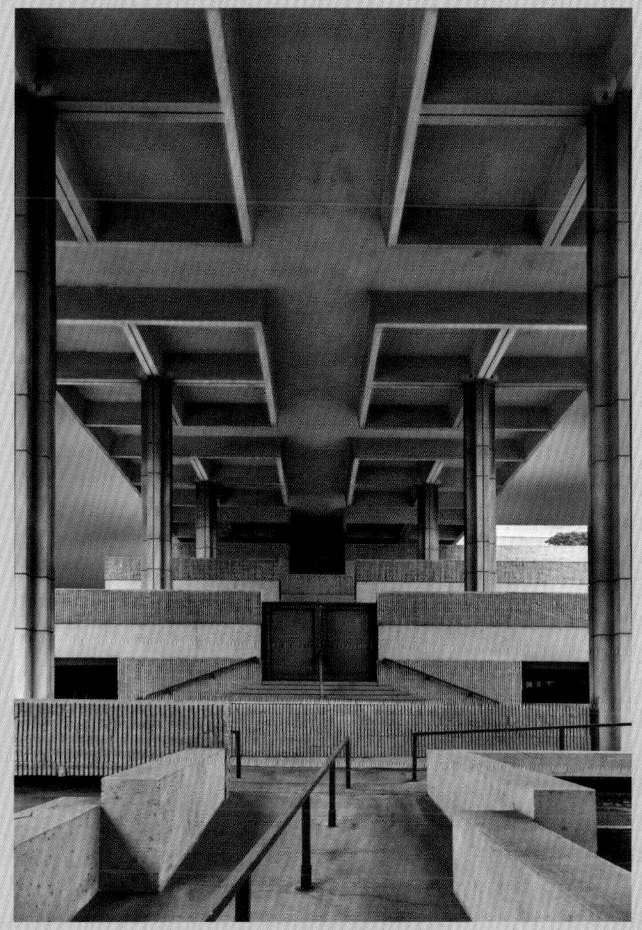

Courthouse Steps, Antony Zacharias, 2011

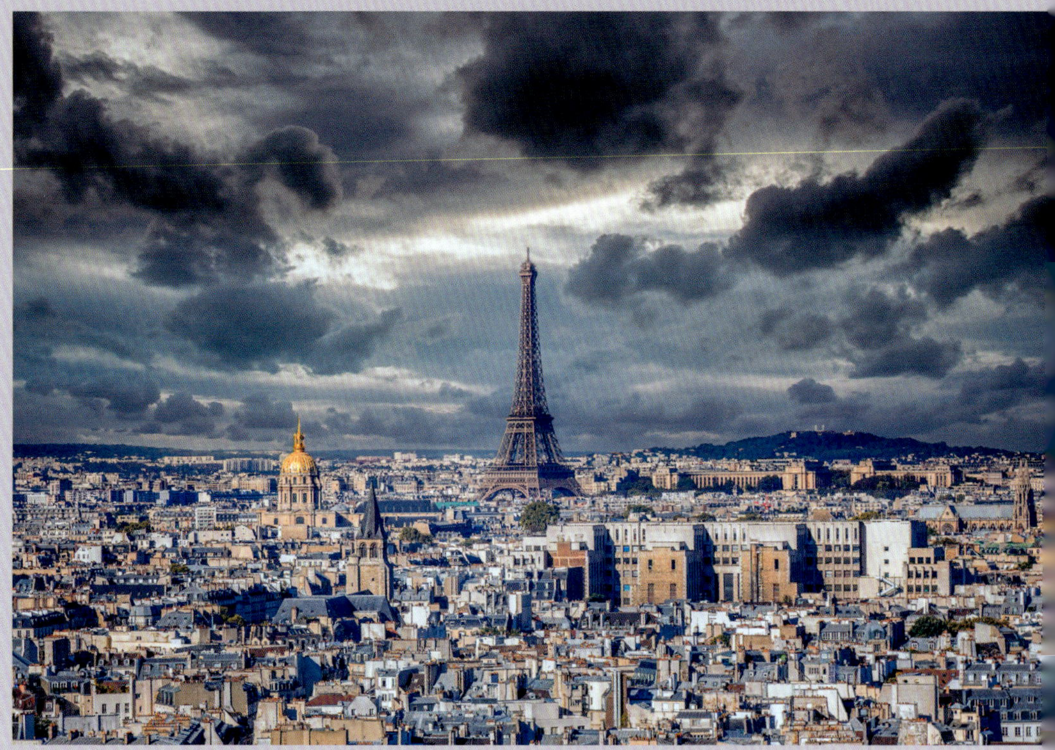

Paris, Antony Zacharias, 2015

EXAGGERATED PERSPECTIVES

DISTORT SPACE TO AMPLIFY VISUAL DRAMA

In this image, the Parisian cityscape is captured from a high vantage point, revealing a dense patchwork of buildings, rooftops and windows that seem to extend endlessly.[1] This wide, elevated view not only highlights the sheer volume of structures, but also compresses them in a way that magnifies the sense of a crowded city. What could easily be a chaotic architectural cluster becomes an intricate composition of shapes and colours, with each overlapping form contributing to the impression that this urban sprawl continues well beyond the frame.[2] The perspective feels almost surreal, as if we're looking at a miniature model rather than a real city. This tension between reality and abstraction is part of what makes exaggerated perspectives so compelling in a maximalist context, as it allows the familiar to be seen in an entirely new way.

Perspective naturally shapes the way we perceive depth, scale and spatial relationships in an image. When these are exaggerated, the viewer becomes deeply engaged with the image, drawn in by how they interpret the elements contained within it. You can achieve this exaggeration by playing with scale, angles, vantage points and focal lengths to intensify feelings of depth and complexity in the image. Rather than capturing a scene from eye-level, look for ways to stretch or compress the visual space so that every detail feels heightened. This could mean shooting from a very high or low angle or employing techniques that distort the viewer's sense of distance.

Working with exaggerated perspectives often involves carefully considering your lens choice and position. A wide-angle lens can expand the foreground and push the background away, making near objects appear disproportionately large. Conversely, a telephoto lens compresses distances, stacking elements on top of one another so that a dense urban scene looks even more crowded and layered.

Exaggerated perspectives also offer a chance to play with scale. Choosing an alternative angle of view or enhancing depth and distortion can prompt a fresh look at a subject or scene. In a maximalist frame where many elements are competing for attention, a unique perspective can help to guide the viewer's eye towards key areas.[3] As a style that thrives on visual abundance, exaggerating perspective becomes a way to fit even more into the frame without losing the intimacy of the smaller details that make up an important part of the story.

[1] *See* Breaking the Edges pp. 72–3
[2] *See* Overlap pp. 22–3
[3] *See* Organized Chaos pp. 16–17

LIGHT, COLOUR AND CONTRAST

HIGH KEY

OVEREXPOSE TO REDUCE DISTRACTION

High-key lighting is often associated with a clean, bright aesthetic, characterized by an abundance of light that reduces contrast and softens shadows. High-key maximalist photography combines this bright, airy quality with an excess of detail and texture. Instead of relying on deep shadows and intense contrast, bright tones, soft diffused light and gentle gradations are used to fill the frame, introducing a layer of complexity that works to accentuate the vibrancy, texture and detail. By employing high-key lighting in maximalist compositions, you can maintain the chaos and richness throughout, while also including a sense of brightness and clarity that enhances the viewer's experience.

It can be challenging to maintain the spirit of maximalism – the idea that every part of the image holds something of interest – while also embracing the characteristics of high-key lighting. It's a balancing act where subtle shifts in tone and texture are essential for keeping the photograph rich and engaging.

In this image, the shape and form of the snow-lined tree stretches across the pale cloudy sky. Its trunk and branches blend into the background, but the photograph doesn't feel empty or devoid of detail. Rather, it draws the eye to the delicate network of branches, inviting closer inspection of their every twist and turn. The high-key effect enhances the tree's structure by reducing the presence of heavy shadows, which allows the intricate lines of each branch and subtle variations in tone to emerge in a gentle, ethereal way. Despite its minimal contrast, an image can still be full of visual information, just presented in a lighter, more subdued manner.

Achieving this effect often involves overexposing your image slightly, while taking care to preserve detail in the highlights and midtones. In a maximalist frame, there might be numerous elements competing for attention, but a high-key approach can unify them by filing the scene with a soft, even light. Textures will become more delicate and shadows less pronounced. In colour images, the palette can take on an almost monochromatic feel, allowing form and line to do much of the work.[1] The key is to check your camera's histogram or exposure levels to avoid losing essential information in the highlight areas – you want these areas to be bright, not featureless.

[1] *See* Emotive Colour pp. 48–9

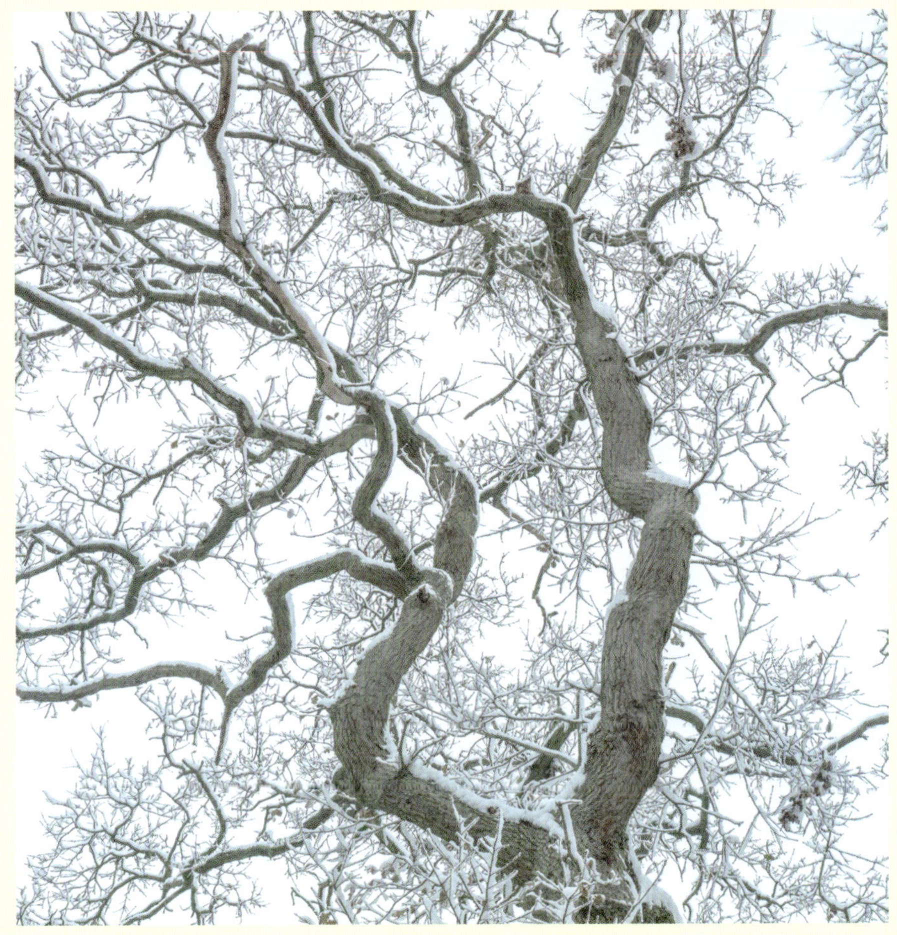

Snowline, Antony Zacharias, 2020

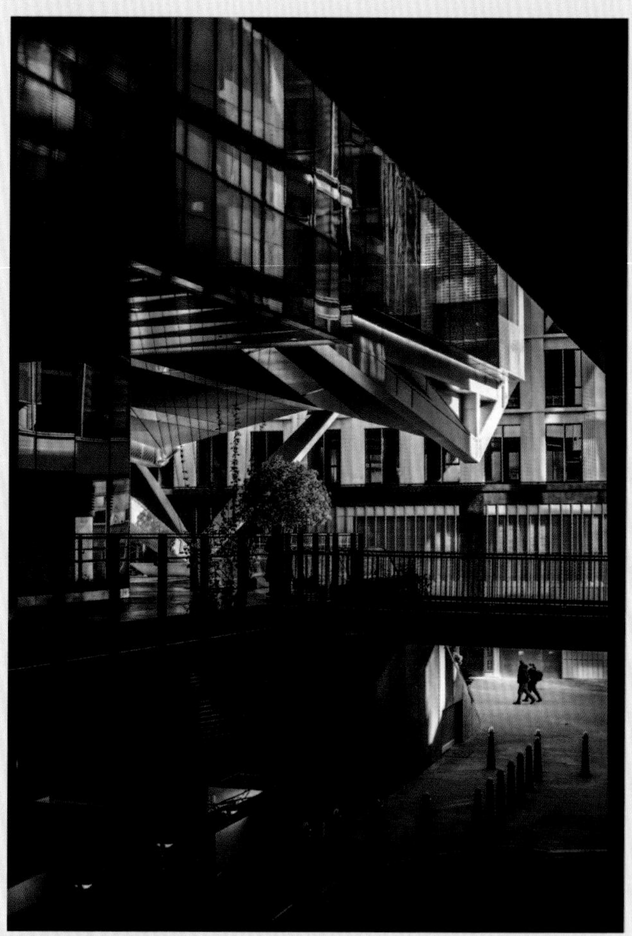

Passing Through, Antony Zacharias, 2022

LOW KEY

DARKEN THE FRAME TO FOCUS ATTENTION

Low-key photographs are usually associated with darkness and deep tones, with minimal areas of brightness. At first, it may seem contradictory to pair this with maximalist photography, which is often defined by visual richness and complexity. However, the concepts can work together to create emotive and layered images.

Rather than reducing detail, low-key lighting reframes it, allowing texture, shape and subtle colour to emerge through contrast and shadow. This subdued lighting introduces a sense of intimacy, drama and mystery, enhancing the emotional atmosphere of a maximalist composition. The result often feels more immersive, drawing the viewer in to explore the scene slowly.

Instead of relying on an even spread of shadow, colour and light, low-key maximalism utilizes deep shadows and selective illumination to reveal multiple layers of detail in the image.[1] The goal is not to reduce the amount of content in the scene, just to control the brightness used to reveal it. Deep shadows become a compositional tool, creating depth and intrigue, while maintaining the complexity that defines maximalism. An image will still have plenty of texture, shape and form, but it is revealed with subtlety.

In this image, the complex architectural setting is concealed in shadow. Strong lines and intersecting planes dominate the frame, hinting at multiple levels and walkways. Initially, the scene seems hidden in darkness, but a closer look uncovers subtle reflections and beams of light that reveal details in the building and surrounding scene. The two people walking through the bright areas add a fleeting sense of movement to the predominantly shadowy environment.[2]

Generally speaking, the light should selectively illuminate key areas in a low-key image, acting as a guide for the eye. The spaces of darkness should work together with the brighter areas to create a unified image. To achieve this effect, identify the stronger shapes or lines in your scene and allow them to emerge from the shadows. If you focus on a few key areas to ensure that the viewer has a starting point from which to begin exploring the frame, they will naturally start to discover the smaller details that slowly begin to appear.

As a lot of the image will be dark, highlights will draw immediate attention, so try to balance the brighter areas: too many can dilute the mood and effect, while too few can simply result in an image that looks underexposed.[3]

[1] *See* Shadows pp. 38–9
[2] *See* Framing pp. 66–7
[3] *See* Contrast pp. 56–7

SHADOWS

CREATE MYSTERY WITH LIGHT AND SHADE

In *Hidden in Plain Sight*, complex shadows introduce vibrant layers of depth into the composition. A palm leaf fills the frame, backlit by sunlight and glowing a vivid green. The light creates an intricate array of shadows from the surrounding plants, overlaying lines and shapes onto the leaf.[1] This layered effect transforms a simple natural form into something unexpectedly abstract and visually rich. A small lizard casts a defined shadow, adding a focal point that enhances the sense of scale and narrative – a quiet moment within a lush, living environment.[2]

Shadows are a powerful way to add layers of depth and intrigue to your scenes. They can become dynamic elements in their own right, creating elaborate patterns that help amplify the complexity of the visual experience. Rather than merely filling space, shadows can become important elements that help draw the viewer deeper into an image; they can become focal points that add contrast and structure to a dense, rich composition.

When an image has multiple layers of interest, complex shadows have the potential to offer an additional layer for the viewer to explore. Their shapes and contours can echo other elements in the frame, tying areas together and helping to direct attention to key areas. Rather than overwhelming the scene, shadows can help make a composition feel intentional and dynamic.

Incorporating shadows effectively into a composition requires careful attention to the available light, especially its direction and intensity. Soft, diffused light will create subtle shadows that can form wonderful shapes, while strong, directional light will lead to striking bold silhouettes and sharper patterns and forms. Both types of light offer unique opportunities to play with visual tone and structure. In particular, low, angled sunlight can cast long, stretched shadows that weave across the frame and interact with other elements in unexpected ways.

Introducing complex shadows into a composition can not only provide visual interest, but also provide your images with an additional narrative layer. Shadows in silhouetted form can introduce mysterious characters and shapes that suggest there are stories unfolding just outside the frame. These visual suggestions invite a deeper engagement with the viewer, encouraging them to imagine a broader narrative beyond that which is immediately visible.

[1] *See* Patterns pp. 25–8
[2] *See* Quiet Moments pp. 90–3

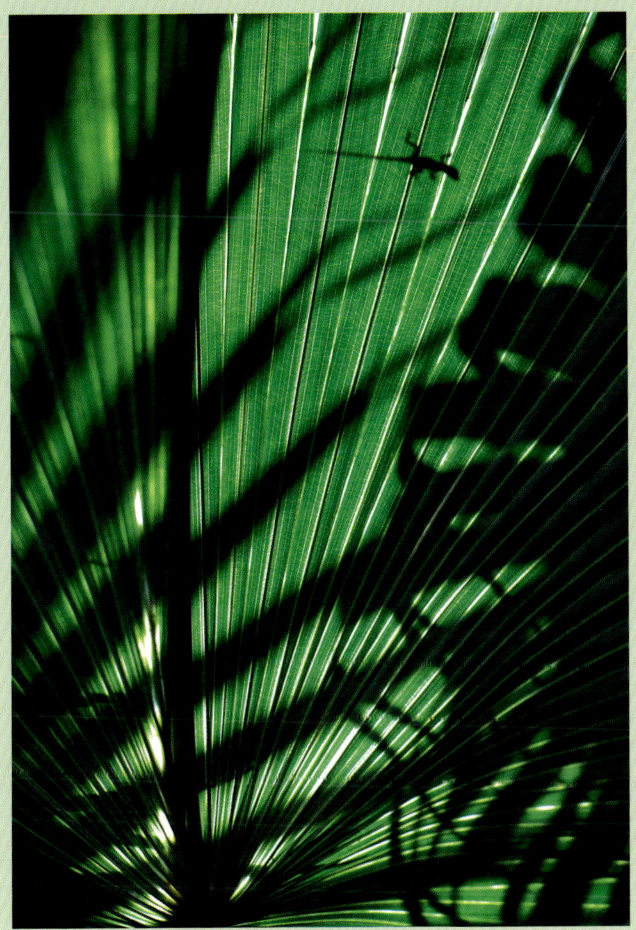

Hidden in Plain Sight, Antony Zacharias, 2011

SHADOWS

In Sarah van Rij's image, *Los Angeles*, this sense of ambiguity and emotional depth is masterfully captured in an urban setting. Strong shadows cast by unknown figures create dramatic silhouettes that are uniquely positioned to tell part of the story. They interact with the architecture and textures in the background, adding tension to the unfolding drama. Each silhouette becomes a point of intrigue that prompts questions about who these individuals might be and what is transpiring beyond the frame.[3]

The vivid red wall provides a bold contrast that intensifies both the clarity and emotional weight of the shadows. This interplay between vibrant colour and sharp silhouette amplifies the visual drama and creates a layered narrative. Viewers are invited not just to observe, but to imagine the relationships, emotions and unseen moments that might have led to this arrangement of light and shadow.

To effectively capture complex shadows in a maximalist context, it is important to observe how the light interacts with the surrounding environment. This can involve anticipating how shadows might shift as moving elements pass through the frame or the position of the light source changes. Patience is key – you need to be prepared to wait for the 'perfect' alignment of subject, shadow and context to help tell your story.[4] By carefully controlling the exposure, clarity and definition will be retained in the shadowed areas, ensuring that the complexity of the shapes remains striking and impactful.

Post-production can help you subtly enhance the shadows in your images and emphasize their intricacies without diminishing their organic feel. Small adjustments to contrast and clarity can be all that is needed to accentuate their forms without overwhelming the balance of your composition.

[3] *See* Breaking the Edges pp. 72–3
[4] *See* Multiple Narratives pp. 110–11

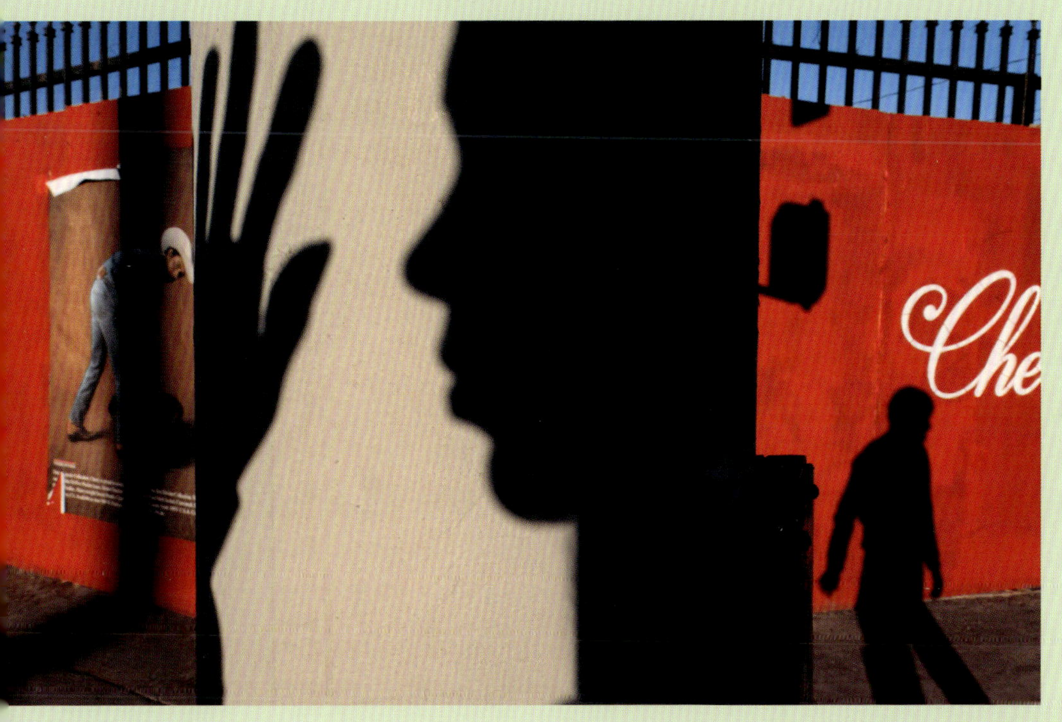

Los Angeles, Sarah van Rij, 2022

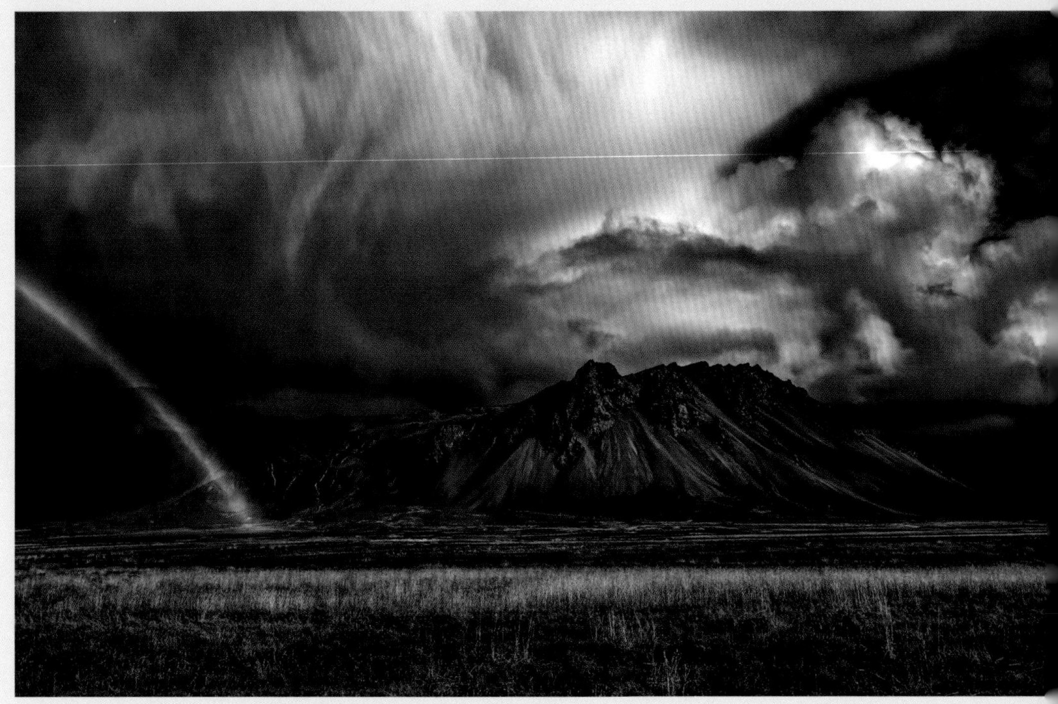

Shadows of the Sky, Antony Zacharias, 2016

DYNAMIC LIGHTING

ENERGIZE THE SCENE WITH ILLUMINATION

This image demonstrates how dynamic lighting can inject energy into a maximalist frame, transforming a visually dense scene into a cohesive and compelling narrative. The bold contrasts between the illuminated storm clouds and the darkened mountain evoke a sense of motion and unpredictability, while the grasses in the foreground, the faint arc of a rainbow and the rugged texture of the rock contribute to a richly layered environment.[1] Despite the visual overload, the shifting light unifies the composition, guiding the viewer's eye across the frame and revealing the interplay between each element. The light becomes an active force within the image, adding depth, tension and a cinematic quality.

Incorporating dynamic lighting into your photographs can add an additional layer of interest to a complex scene. This approach can transform visual chaos into something captivating, as each ray of light highlights texture, shape and other elements that might otherwise go unnoticed. Whether it is natural sunlight filtering through trees, or artificial light in a studio or urban environment, dynamic light is rarely flat or even. It is these scattered areas of brightness that serve as natural focal points that can be used to guide the viewer through a scene.

Carefully controlling the exposure is vital, as you want to avoid areas that are overexposed to the point of losing detail, while ensuring sufficient information remains visible in the shadow areas. If in doubt, slightly underexpose, as shadow detail can be recovered more easily in post-production. Alternatively, bracketing your images (taking multiple frames at different exposure settings) can be helpful when there are extreme variations between the lighter and darker areas, enabling you to create a composite image that contains the best parts of each exposure.

When incorporating dynamic lighting, it is important to consider the angle and intensity of the light source, as the direction of the light will have a profound impact on how it interacts with the textures, objects and details in the frame. If you position key elements where the light is strongest, this will enhance the impression of power and energy, so try to let the light interact with the environment in a way that amplifies the details you have chosen to include; subtle changes in position can transform the emotion of an image.

Colour temperature and white balance also play a role in dynamic lighting, especially when there are multiple light sources, so you should consider how warmer or cooler tones affect a scene. This will become much more pronounced when your composition contains vibrant, colourful elements.

[1] *See* Contrast pp. 56–7

LONG EXPOSURE

LAYER TIME TO REVEAL MOTION

Long exposures capture not just what is seen, but what is continually unfolding. Instead of photographing a moment, it allows motion and atmosphere to be captured in a single, dynamic, layered image. In a maximalist context – where the frame is often already full of detailed visual information – long exposures can increase the visual complexity, bringing both clarity and ambiguity to the frame.

In a well-executed long exposure in low-light conditions, even seemingly sparse environments can create successful maximalist images, filled with visual complexity. Light trails, illuminated architecture, stars, reflective surfaces and subtle gradients will all contribute to a fuller image that reveals not just what is there, but what is happening continuously.[1]

In *Stellar Communications*, a field of radio satellite dishes is captured beneath a sky full of star trails. The long exposure reveals the rotation of the Earth itself, capturing the stars' paths in the sky, while the darkened land below remains still and sharp. The sweeping light trails stretch beyond the edges of the frame, hinting at the vastness of the universe and the endless motion that continues beyond the visible.[2] The image's density contributes to its maximalist context, which does not have a single focal point, but instead invites the viewer to take in the whole scene and revel in the wonders of the night sky.[3]

A long exposure is not only a creative decision. It can also be a practical one, especially in low-light conditions where there is no other choice but to extend the exposure time to enable an adequate exposure. However, it is always a question of balance, as a longer exposure will introduce movement into the frame: too much movement can blur important details, but too short an exposure can underexpose the scene. Using a higher ISO can help here, but this needs to be balanced against the increased digital noise it might introduce.

On a practical level, a tripod is essential for keeping the static elements sharp, while your choice of shutter speed determines the appearance of the trails and blurs created by moving subjects. It is up to you to decide how long you want the trails to be, which parts of the scene should remain in sharp focus and how much blur feels right for the story you're telling. As this is unique to each scene – and your personal preferences – you will need to experiment with your exposure time to see what works best for you.

[1] *See* Multiple Focal Points pp. 20–1
[2] *See* Breaking the Edges pp. 72–3
[3] *See* Quiet Moments pp. 90–3

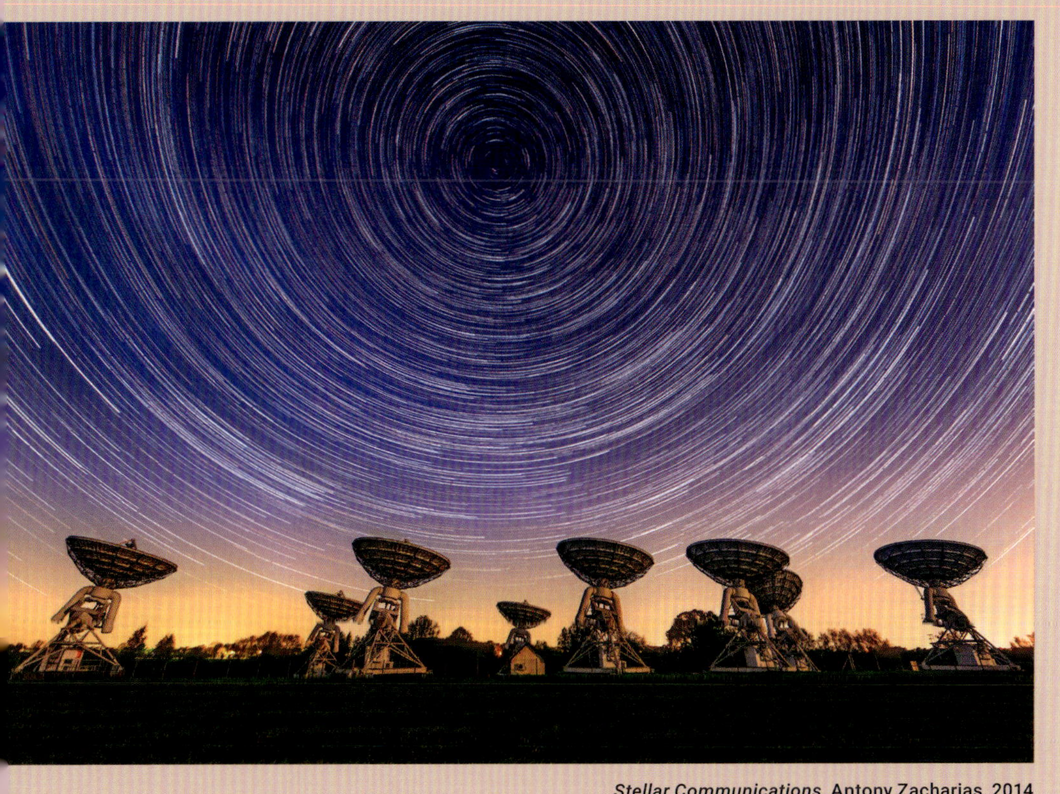

Stellar Communications, Antony Zacharias, 2014

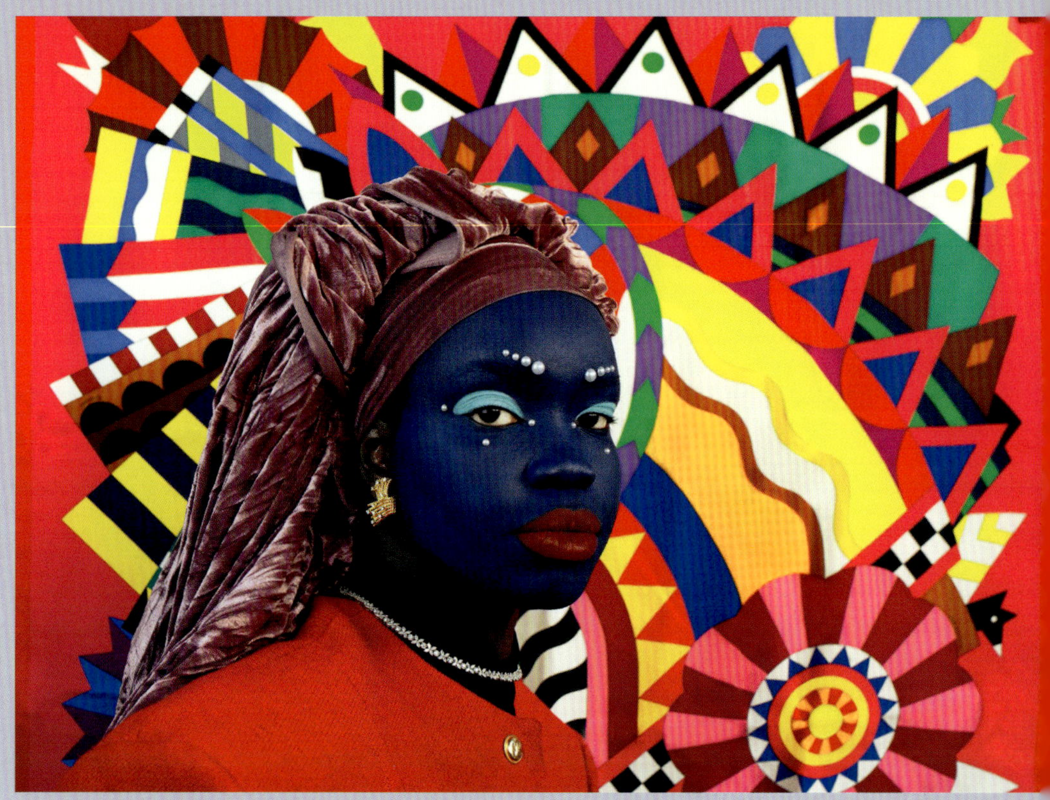

Blue Face, Atong Atem, 2021

EXPLOSIVE COLOUR

INCREASE INTENSITY WITH SATURATED COLOUR

In this image, the background bursts with angular patterns and vibrant hues, creating a strong sense of movement and visual energy.[1] The subject's deep-blue-painted skin and red lipstick transform her into both a striking focal point and a continuation of the vivid designs behind her. Her piercing gaze anchors the viewer, providing a moment of stillness within the colourful visual chaos. Here, colour doesn't merely decorate the frame, it heightens the narrative and challenges the viewer to engage with every inch of the image.[2]

When incorporating intense colour palettes, the idea is to purposely crowd the frame with as many bold tones as possible. Include as many clashing colours as you can, trusting that the overall energy will unify the scene. This will create an image with a unique visual strength, where each colour intensifies the next and the image feels full of life.

However, a key challenge is avoiding chaos. It is important to ensure that there is still an underlying sense of rhythm or order, despite the overload of colour. One effective technique is to cluster colours in certain areas so there is a sense of structure to the frame. This doesn't have to be a rigid grouping or positioning, just enough of a guide to help the viewer navigate through the deluge of colour. Repeating patterns, shapes or other elements can all be used to create a visual pathway to guide the eye. The vibrant, bold colours should feel exciting and energetic to the viewer, while at the same time coherent and balanced.

Lighting will play a significant role. Bright, even lighting will ensure each colour is displayed at its full intensity, while shadows or darker areas can reduce the vibrancy of certain colours, potentially creating a visual imbalance.

During post-production, avoid the temptation to over edit the scene. Increasing the vibrancy and saturation too far can result in an artificial look that detracts from the image's authenticity. It's often best to start with a scene that's already naturally vibrant and use editing to enhance rather than overwhelm. Selective editing, where specific areas of colour are boosted individually, can create focal points that prevent the image from becoming monotonous in its intensity. The goal is to highlight the most compelling aspects of your palette without reducing the scene to a uniformly bright spectacle.

[1] *See* Patterns pp. 25–8
[2] *See* Portraits pp. 112–15

EMOTIVE COLOUR

EXPRESS FEELINGS THROUGH COLOUR

Colour can play a huge part in shaping the composition in maximalist photographs, where everything is often exaggerated, dynamic and bursting with energy. However, colour isn't just about catching the viewer's attention – it can also be an emotional and symbolic tool within the complexity of a maximalist image. The thoughtful use of colour can evoke strong feelings that resonate with an audience, stirring personal memories that will lead to a deeper engagement with the photograph.

In *Carousel*, a carnival horse adorned with vivid paintwork and intricate details stands out against a background of golden lights and ornate patterns. The swirling shapes and elaborate decorations embody the essence of maximalism, but the combination of colours – the golden tones and soft pastels – introduce strong feelings to the scene. Their cheerful, nostalgic quality immediately draws the eye, suggesting the excitement of a fairground, childhood wonder or a fleeting moment of celebration.[1] Even though the scene is filled with visual information, the warm tones help to unify the composition and invite the viewer to share in that sense of joyful chaos.[2] Colour isn't just a visual tool, but also a powerful emotional cue.

To infuse emotion into a maximalist image, it helps to consider how different colours interact with one another. Red is often associated with passion, danger and urgency, while yellow evokes warmth, optimism and energy. Cooler tones, such as blue and green, can introduce a sense of calm, serenity or mystery.

The key to using emotive colour in a maximalist setting is to prevent it from becoming overwhelming. With so many elements in an image, the combination can easily become overpowering, so consider how colours can provide a pleasing contrast and area of respite to the intensity of a scene. For example, when cooler tones are used alongside more intense colours in a maximalist photograph, they can provide a visual counterbalance, helping to diffuse the intensity and offer the viewer a resting space within the chaos.

A strong pop of colour will stand out even more if it's set against a quieter background, while multiple bold tones can coexist if they share similar brightness or saturation levels. Additionally, the strength and vibrancy of the colours themselves will have a pronounced effect: bright reds will energize a scene, whereas pastel pinks are less intense and create a dreamy, nostalgic quality.

[1] *See* Nostalgia pp. 98–9
[2] *See* Wonder and Delight pp. 94–7

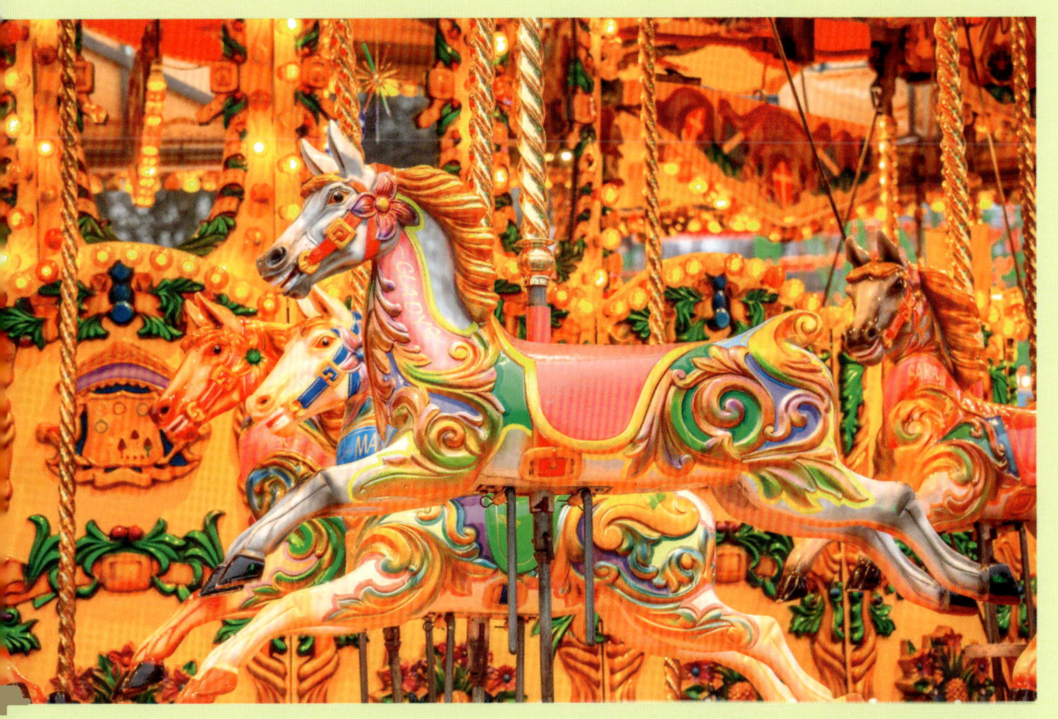

Carousel, Antony Zacharias, 2019

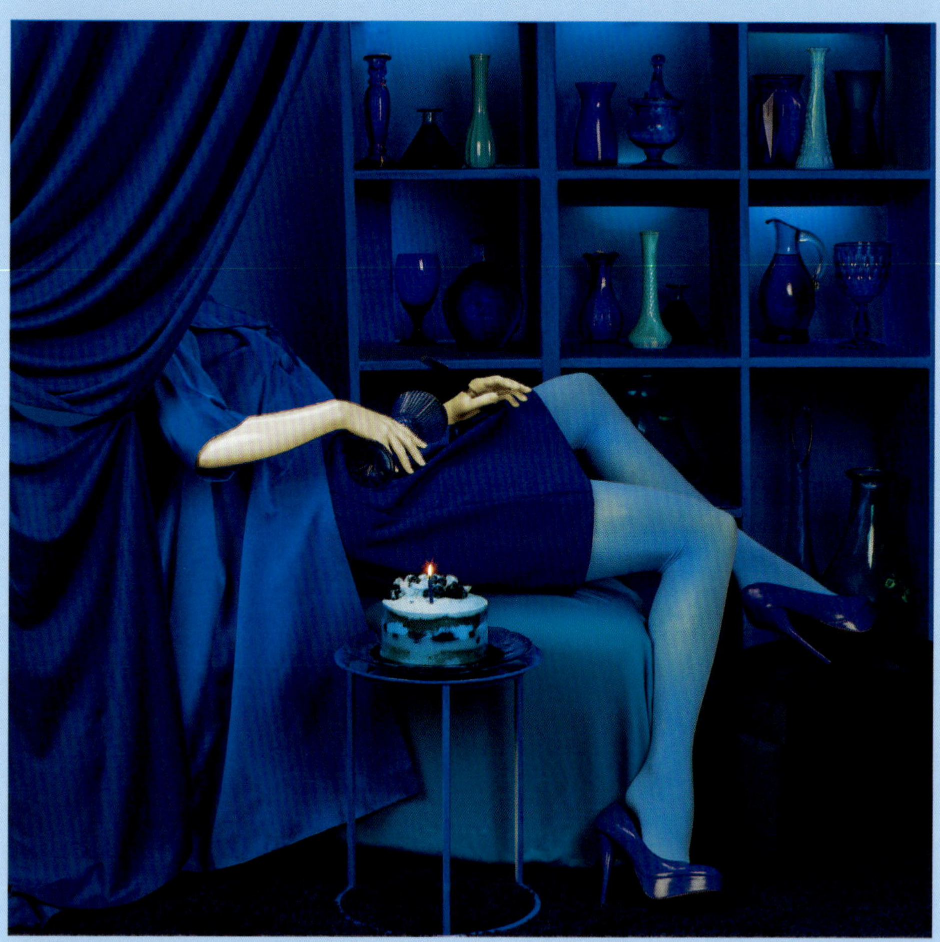

Birthday Blues, Patty Carroll, 2021

MONOCHROME

USE LESS COLOUR AND MORE FOCUS

Instead of relying on a wide range of colours and tones, monochromatic maximalist compositions retain a similar energy through the combination of depth, texture and complexity found in the subtle differences or shades of a single colour. The chosen colour palette will become imposing when allowed to dominate the scene, controlling the energy and atmosphere, and ultimately the emotion and narrative of the photograph.[1]

Patty Carroll's image uses similar blue tones throughout the frame, yet despite its limited colour palette, the scene feels anything but sparse. The luxurious folds of fabric, layered curtains and matching vases and glassware create a sumptuous, almost theatrical atmosphere. The statue-like figure in the centre is draped in fabric of the same hue and merges seamlessly with the backdrop, giving the impression that the person is both part of the setting and the main focal point.[2]

This underscores one of monochrome maximalism's key strengths: the unification of subject and environment. Because the colour remains consistent throughout, each element stands out primarily through texture, shape and light, which draws attention to smaller details that might otherwise be overshadowed by competing colours. A monochrome palette can also prevent the viewer from feeling overwhelmed by the complexity of the image, as a single dominant colour can simplify the visual chaos and offer a clear point of focus.

In a monochromatic scene, the impact of light and shadow becomes significantly more pronounced. Light helps to carve out shapes, emphasize texture and create a sense of depth.[3] The limited palette heightens these contrasts, drawing attention to the colour and detail.

When working on your own monochrome maximalist photographs, start by choosing a colour that resonates with the mood you want to evoke. This is naturally easier to control in a studio environment, but it's not impossible to find outdoor scenes that are dominated by your chosen colour. Once you have settled on a hue, gather objects and materials that fit within its broad range – some might be slightly lighter or darker, while others may have subtle variations that add depth. Fabric, textures, decorative items and even lighting gels can help you maintain consistency. If you're shooting a portrait, encourage your subject to wear clothing that aligns with the chosen colour, so they become a coherent part of the composition.[4]

[1] *See* Emotive Colour pp. 48–9
[2] *See* Surrealism pp. 102–5
[3] *See* Textures pp. 74–5
[4] *See* Portraits pp. 112–15

BLACK AND WHITE

HIGHLIGHT ABUNDANCE WITHOUT COLOUR

This image may initially overwhelm with its density of information – the tangled branches and roots, textured tree trunks and overlapping grasses. However, in black and white the complexity appears to have more structure and order, with the highlights and shadows working together to separate overlapping elements. The reflections on the water create an almost surreal symmetry that amplifies the depth and complexity of the composition, guiding the eye deeper into the frame.[1] The central focal point – an alligator gliding stealthily through the water – emerges as an understated, yet powerful presence, which enhances the narrative and suggests hidden tension. The lack of colour also draws attention to texture and form, which helps bring structure to the image where repeated patterns and shapes appear.[2]

Black-and-white images encourage a more intentional viewing experience. The viewer is drawn to examine the image closely, guided by contrast and shapes, rather than the immediate impact of colour.[3]

When composing black-and-white images that are rich in detail, seek out scenes where there is dynamic light, and shadow and contrast.[4] [5] These can be used to draw attention and create interest throughout the frame, instead of relying on colour to highlight elements. Assessing the range of available tones becomes crucial – the deepest blacks can help anchor the composition, while the brightest whites can push specific areas into focus. A strong maximalist black-and-white photograph will often contain a broad range of tones between these two extremes, with a gradation of grey tones that helps bring depth throughout the image.

When it comes to post-processing, dodging (brightening) and burning (darkening) specific areas can help to create or reinforce a visual path though the composition, while small increases to contrast and texture can give shapes more definition and individuality.[6] You may also want to consider reducing the clarity in certain areas to soften transitions between elements. This can help guide the viewer's eye and create a more cohesive, atmospheric feel, although it is crucial that you maintain the overall balance – nothing should seem overly processed.

[1] *See* Symmetry pp. 28–9
[2] *See* Repetition pp. 70–1
[3] *See* Shape and Geometry pp. 78–9
[4] *See* Contrast pp. 56–7
[5] *See* Dynamic Lighting pp. 40–43
[6] *See* Textures pp. 74–5

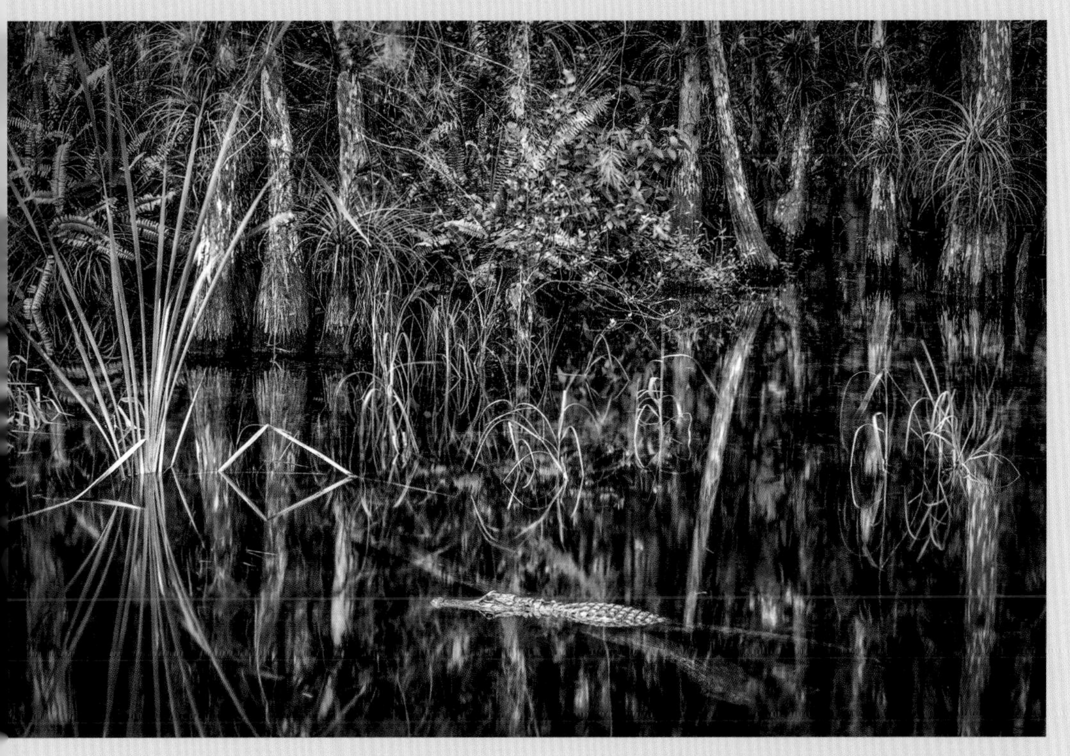

Stillness in the Everglades, Antony Zacharias, 2009

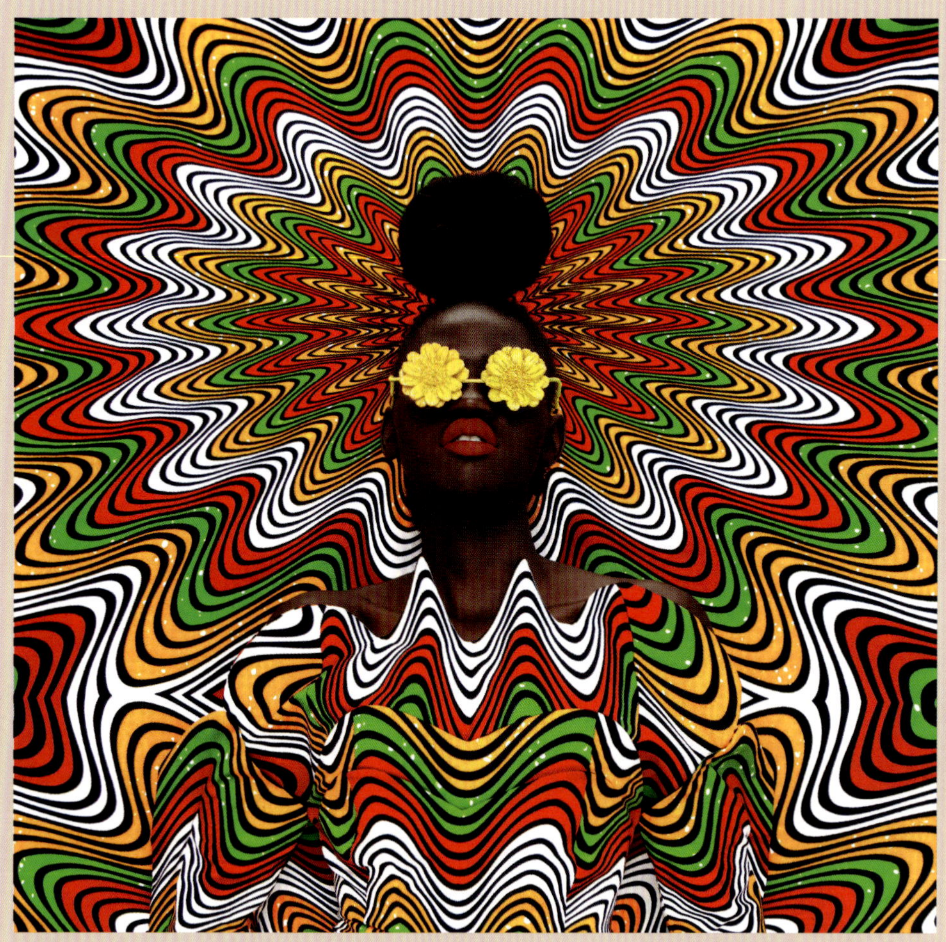

Camo 34, 'The greatest truth is the simplest one.' (African Proverb), Thandiwe Muriu, 2022

PATTERNED COLOUR

REPEAT COLOURS TO UNIFY A SCENE

Patterned colour palettes take the concept of patterns beyond shapes and textures to focus instead on the repetition or arrangement of hues.[1] It refers to the intentional arrangement of colours in a way that creates both rhythm and harmony within an image. In maximalist photography, colour is often the driving force used to grab the viewer's attention. Where the colours form a deliberate pattern, this multiplies the impact, creating an image that not only presents an explosion of colour, but does so in a way that an audience can find mesmerizing. This combination of repetition and variation in colour and texture can unify a complex scene and create a compelling visual experience.[2]

One way to develop a patterned colour palette is to choose a set of complementary tones and distribute them throughout the composition. Alternatively, a monochromatic approach could involve multiple shades of a single colour, arranged in geometric or organic shapes. In either case, the repeated palette anchors the viewer, helping them navigate a maximalist environment where forms and textures fill the frame.

Consider how lighting can amplify or subdue the colourful patterns. Soft, diffused light tends to flatten out differences in tone, which will make any subtle variations stand out more clearly. Conversely, strong directional light can intensify shadows and highlights, which will affect the way colours are perceived. If you're aiming for bold, vibrant colours, then bright, even lighting may be best to ensure that each colour stands out.[3] If necessary, you can fine tune the colour balance or saturation in post-production to accentuate a particular colour, or to ensure that no single tone overwhelms the others.

Thandiwe Muriu's striking portrait of a woman leaps out of the frame.[4] Her outfit, background and even accessories are all adorned in swirling patterns of red, green, yellow and black. Each colour forms wavy lines that appear to pulse outwards from her figure, creating a hypnotic effect. Her sunglasses pick up on the same colour palette, tying her seamlessly into the psychedelic design behind her. Despite the visual complexity, this patterned colour palette unifies the composition through its vibrant hues. The viewer's eye travels from one swirl to the next and the result is captivating rather than chaotic. There is a sense of order among the visual complexity, so the scene appears balanced and unified, yet still holds the energy and intensity of maximalism.

[1] *See* Patterns pp. 24–7
[2] *See* Repetition pp. 70–1
[3] *See* Explosive Colour pp. 46–7
[4] *See* Portraits pp. 112–15

CONTRAST

ADD DRAMA WITH DARKNESS AND LIGHT

Contrast – the variation between the light and dark elements in the frame – is a powerful tool at the maximalist photographer's disposal. Where an image is complex and full of detail, contrast can highlight and organize specific elements, create dramatic effects and guide the viewer through the frame. It is not merely about the differences between black and white tones, but the variations in light, colour and texture that all contribute to give a maximalist image visual impact.

In this photograph, a sweeping field of hay bales contrasts with the dramatic sky, highlighting how the light and shadow interact in a black-and-white setting. Each bale stands out as a distinct shape against the lighter rows spread throughout the field. The turbulent sky reveals a broad range of tones, from near-black storm clouds to radiant beams of sunlight breaking through.[1] This duality draws attention to both the land and the sky, allowing the viewer to move between the repetition of the hay bales and the drama overhead.[2] Even though there's a lot to look at in the scene, the variation in brightness ensures that each layer of detail demands attention and doesn't get lost in the overall image.

The ability to use contrast to bring clarity and impact to a maximalist photograph results in the creation of images that are not necessarily balanced evenly, but that isn't the goal here. The use of strong tonal differences can guide the viewer through a complex scene and ensure they have a visual path to follow. This framework allows each element of a scene to be appreciated in its own right, while still contributing to an overall sense of abundance.

In a black-and-white image, positioning bright and dark elements close to one another creates visual points that are obvious for the audience. In a colour image, a similar effect can be achieved by pairing vibrant hues with muted or darker tones. In either case, the key to using contrast in a maximalist image starts with an awareness of the light source and the direction it is hitting the subject. Harsh sunlight (or dramatic cloud cover, as in this image) will produce pronounced shadows and bright highlights that naturally create high contrast. In more subdued lighting situations, you may need to seek out areas of brightness and shadow to help emphasize the differences in tonality.

Post-processing can also be used to enhance contrasts captured in an image; deepening blacks can give key shapes a stronger outline, while brightening highlights can draw attention to specific areas. Restraint is paramount, though, and each step should clarify and enhance the structure of the image, not overwhelm it.

[1] *See* Dynamic Lighting pp. 40–3
[2] *See* Repetition pp. 70–1

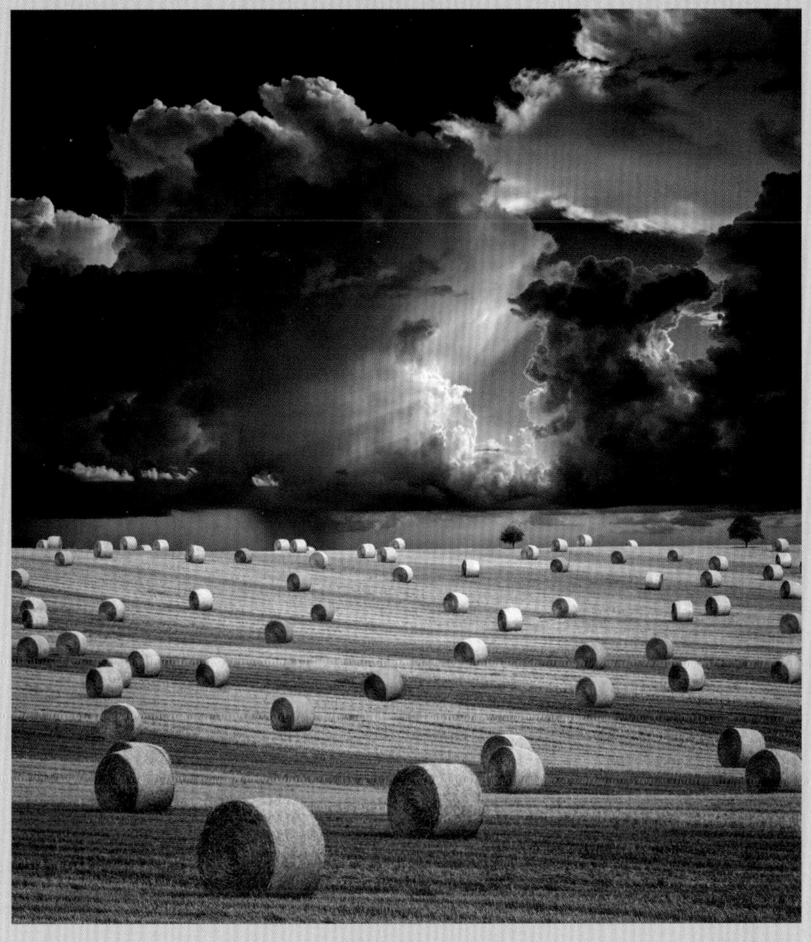

Harvest Storms, Antony Zacharias, 2007

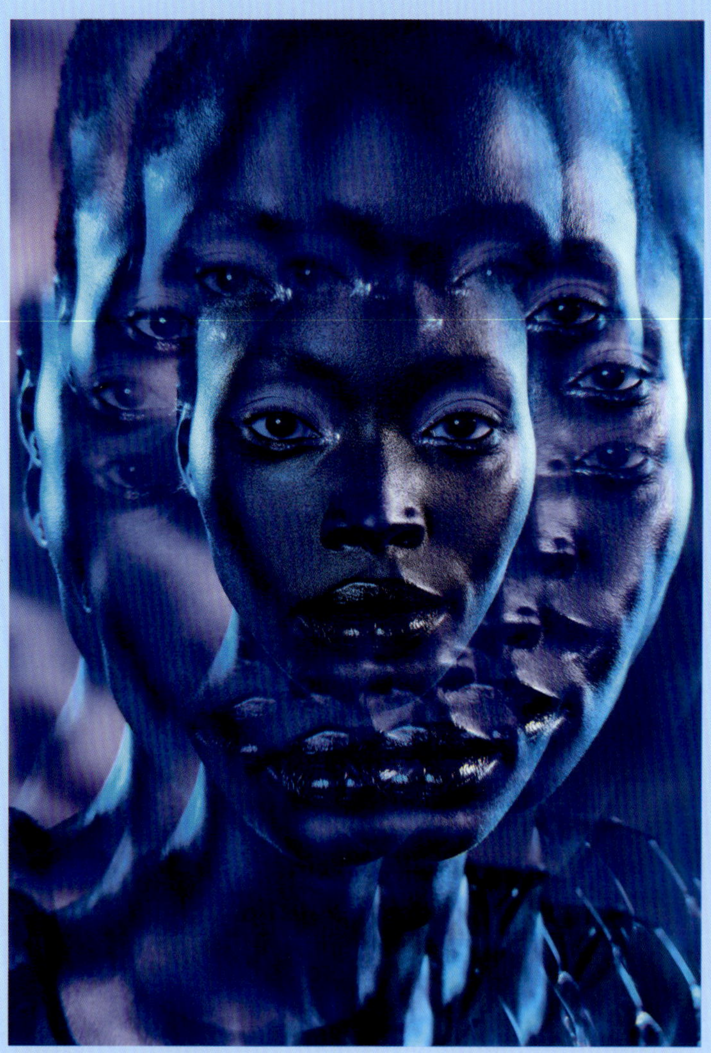

HYPNO, Lindsay Adler, 2024

LAYERS OF COLOUR

BUILD COMPLEXITY WITH COLOUR

Lindsay Adler's photograph, *HYPNO*, commands immediate attention. A single portrait is repeated multiple times, with each version tinted in a shade of electric blue.[1] The arrangement of the overlapping layered faces creates a hypnotic effect that transforms a simple headshot into something compelling and almost futuristic-looking. Despite the repetition and intensity of hues, the photograph retains a sense of unity: the colour blue dominates, anchoring the composition and preventing the overlapping faces from feeling chaotic.

Dramatic layers of colour in a maximalist photograph can add emotional depth, richness and intensity to the composition. The layers refer to the strategic use of multiple (sometimes overlapping) colour elements within a photograph. In maximalism, these coloured layers may be physical elements within the scene, or they might be produced through lighting and exposure techniques.[2] Either technique has the power to transform something familiar into something more surreal, which naturally invites the viewer to explore the subject in new ways.[3]

In maximalist photography, colour layers are not just used to add brightness, but serve to create depth, drama and an additional dimension. However, dramatic colour layers can be overwhelming, and so a considered composition is vital. In a maximalist scene that is already complex and full of detailed information, you don't want the viewer to feel lost or overwhelmed. Consider how the layered hues interact with the other elements in the scene, especially when the broader environment also contains strong colours. One way of achieving this is to use a single dominant hue as your base layer, then layer one or two secondary colours that accentuate key shapes or subjects. This will help guide your viewer through the scene and offer a suggestion of order.

Lighting will of course underpin the appearance of the coloured layers. The lighting for dramatic colour layers pushes the boundaries of what we typically consider 'natural' or balanced lighting. This approach involves stacking or blending multiple colours – usually through coloured gels or creative post-processing – which can result in an image that appears mysterious and exciting.

Editing choices can further enhance or refine these layers. Small boosts to saturation or contrast can make certain colours 'pop', but although the goal is drama, you need to remain mindful of the viewer's experience: if every corner of the frame is competing for attention then it can easily become overpowering, weakening the overall impact.

[1] *See* Portraits pp. 112–15
[2] *See* Multiple Exposure pp. 76–7
[3] *See* Surrealism pp. 102–5

CREATIVE TECHNIQUES

COLLAGE

TELL A STORY IN LAYERS AND FRAGMENTS

Maximalist collage is a dynamic and expressive approach to image-making that incorporates diverse ideas and visual elements to create complex, layered compositions. It celebrates abundance by combining various materials and textures to produce a visual overload through the cutting and layering of elements. Coupled with photography, collage can turn a single image into something far more complex. From a maximalist standpoint, collage enables the creation of complexity from numerous fragments that multiply meaning within the image, where contrast, repetition and accumulation generate an energy and narrative.

Photomontage refers specifically to the physical or digital combination of photographic elements into a single, layered (collaged) image. This may involve cutting and pasting printed photographs, scanning textures, arranging found imagery, assembling fragments in editing software or a combination of these.

An alternative approach involves constructing or staging scenes that imitate the stylistic form of collage, but without the literal layering of materials. These images often exaggerate contrasts in texture, subject, pattern or colour to create the chaotic harmony of collage, even when they are created entirely in-camera or through digital retouching.

What unites these approaches is how the narrative is presented in a fragmented way. Collage-based maximalist photography rarely presents a unified, single-perspective world. Instead, it creates a complex visual blend of elements that may differ in origin, scale or context, but when they are brought together, they form a new and compelling story. The viewer is invited to interpret these overlapping layers and build meaning through the connections, contrasts and spaces between them.

Hannah Höch's collage of a flower bouquet is made up from photographed eyes and patterned paper fragments. It offers a 'true' maximalist photographic collage, which was created by cutting and assembling photographic and printed elements. This results in a surreal composition containing stylized repetition.[1] Each element retains an individuality, yet contributes to a larger, layered composition. Here, the transformed flower is open to multiple interpretations, as petals are replaced with eyes staring back at the viewer. The repeated layers and forms add intensity and weight to the image, enhancing its impact. The viewer is not just observing detail, but is immersed in it and the tension it creates.[2]

[1] *See* Surrealism pp. 102–5
[2] *See* Symbolism pp. 118–21

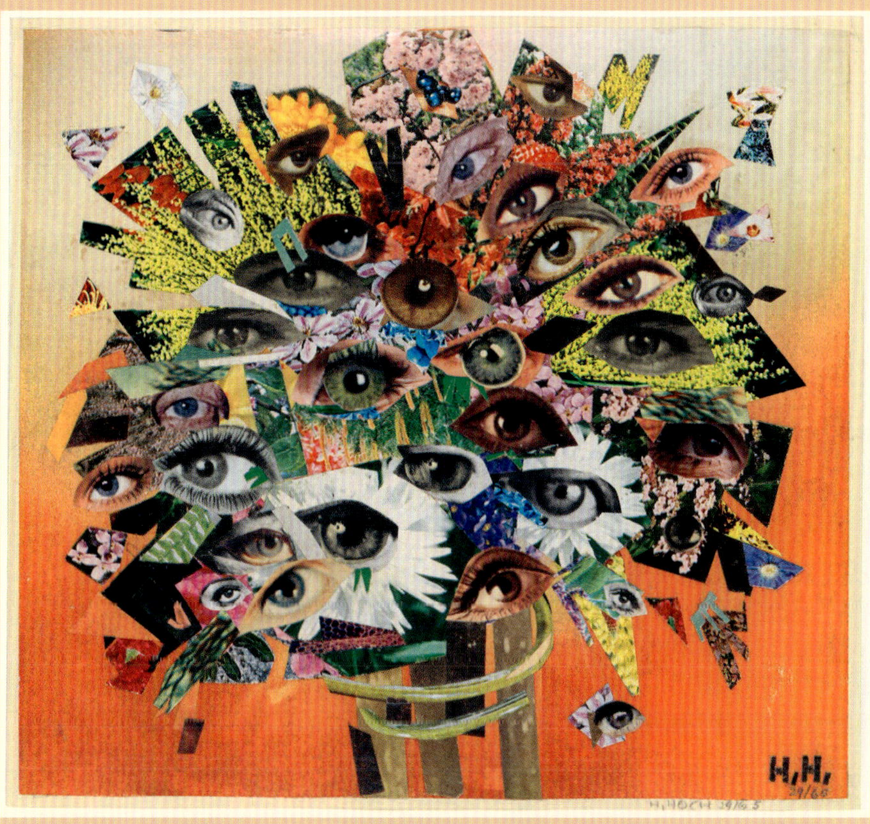

Denkmal der Eitelkeit II, Hannah Höch, 1926

COLLAGE

Mickalene Thomas' more contemporary portrait of a woman in a densely styled, patterned environment applies the collage aesthetic through a staged photograph. Although not a collage in the physical sense, it visually emulates one. Each element in the composition – the choices of fashion, wall-coverings, fabrics and plants – feels like a cutout that has been placed precisely in the frame. It seems as though the subject, Lili, is both part of the scene, yet at the same time, somehow separate from it. There is an obvious tension created between the contrasting elements and clashing textures, and the maximalist qualities of the image are heightened by the density of the visual information and details. There is no negative space – the image is packed with colours, textures, patterns and shapes that retain their individuality yet collide and overlap in the style of a regular collage.

When working with either 'true' collage or collage-inspired compositions, it is essential that you carefully consider the placement of each element within the frame. Don't feel the need to aim for seamless blending, but allow elements to stand alone and retain their individuality. Think in terms of layers – not just visually, but conceptually too. The uniqueness of some objects and how they interact and relate to others may seem unnatural, but it can still be effective if they help tell the story or offer visual clues.[3]

Collage-based photography also requires you to pay close attention to textures and patterns, as these can play an important role in building layers that create a sense of depth and complexity.[4] Textures can be emphasized through digital manipulation in post-production to imitate differences in papers, prints or brushstrokes, or in physical collage incorporating rough or smooth fabrics or prints.[5] Textures and patterns can also be combined to create a sense of contrast, tension and movement within a collage. A highly textured, chaotic area can be juxtaposed with a smoother, more serene section to create a dynamic flow that helps the viewer's eye travel across the composition. This contrast can also add to the layers of complexity.[6]

If you are creating a physical collage and want to produce a single final image, it is important to photograph the work in a way that accurately captures its texture, depth and detail. Avoid harsh, uneven lighting and opt instead for softer, diffused light to help minimize shadows and glare.

[3] *See* Layered Meanings pp. 134–5
[4] *See* Patterns pp. 24–7
[5] *See* Textures pp. 74–5
[6] *See* Juxtaposition pp. 130–1

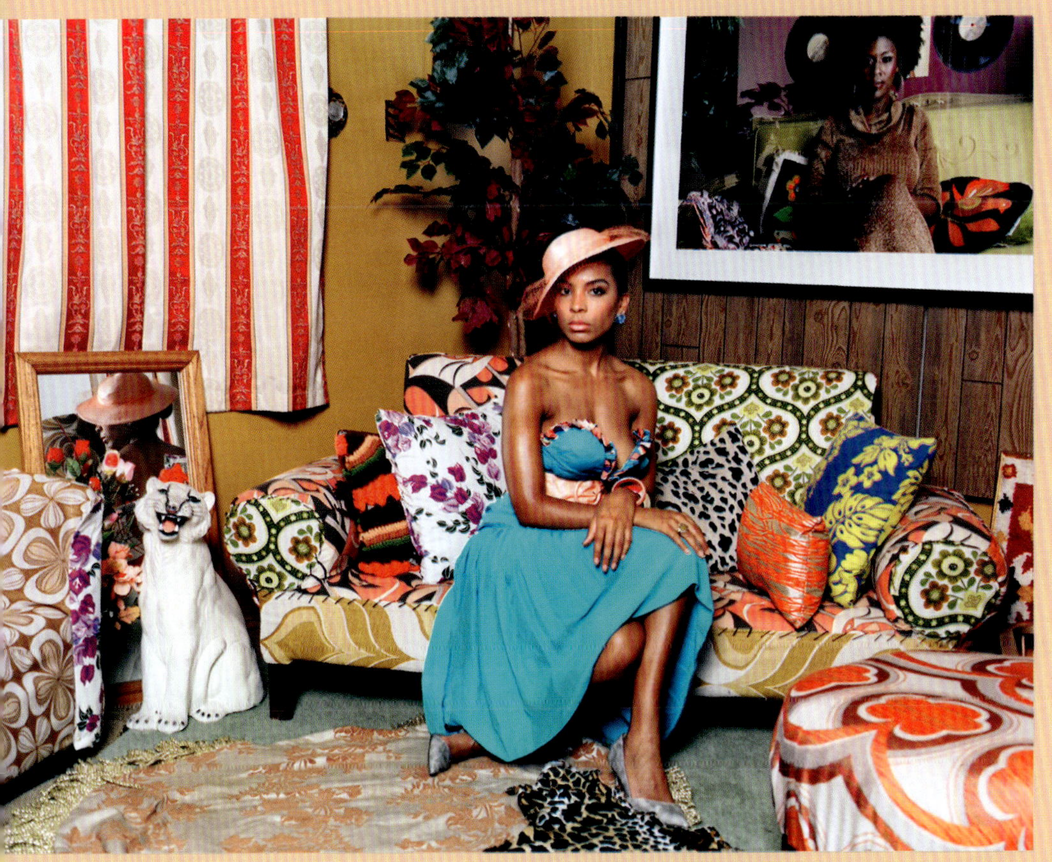

Portrait of Lili in Colour, Mickalene Thomas, 2008

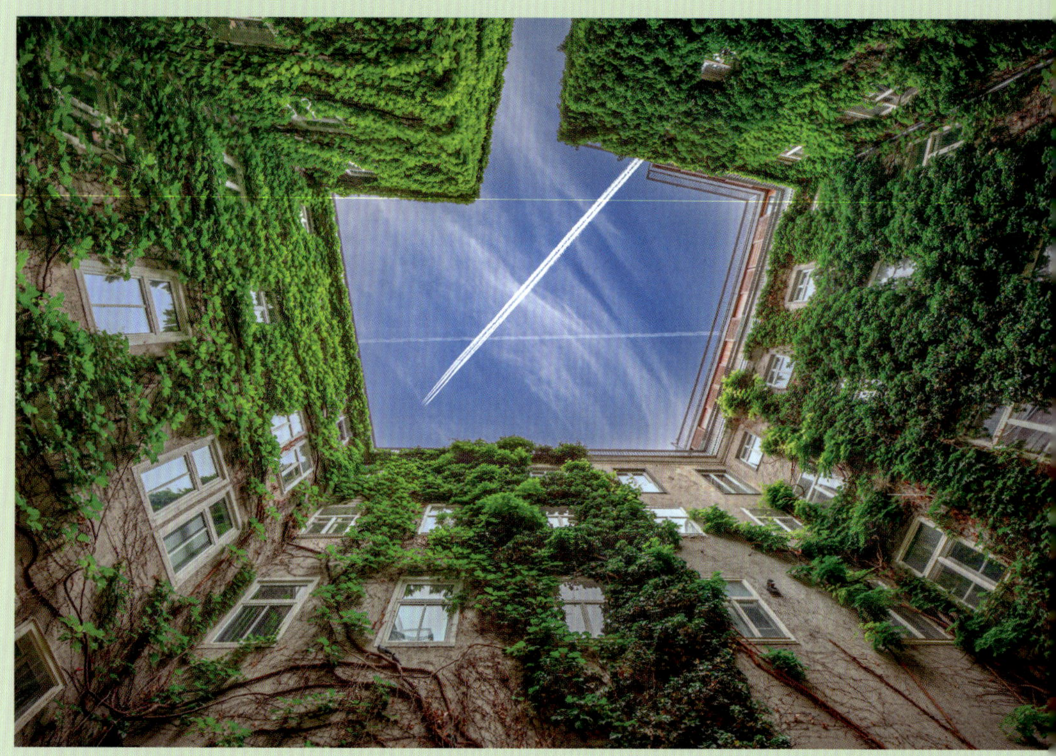

Between the Walls and the Sky, Antony Zacharias, 2022

FRAMING

DEFINE BOUNDARIES TO GUIDE THE EYE

Framing is a helpful way to amplify complexity, create tension and generally heighten the sense of abundance in an image. By choosing to frame your subject within a larger scene, you're guiding the viewer's attention while still leaving space for the surrounding details to tell their own stories. In a maximalist context, framing can bring clarity and intention to a photograph, ensuring that every corner of the image contributes to its overall impact.[1]

One of the most engaging aspects of framing in a busy photograph is how it invites the viewer to explore. In a maximalist image, framing individual elements can lead the viewer to pause and inspect the details to discover what's happening throughout. Here, the vine-covered walls enclose the scene and draw the viewer's gaze upwards towards the sky. The contrast between the organic chaos of the plants and the crisp geometric clarity of the opening above creates tension and balance. The sky, intersected by two vapour trails, provides an additional focal point that grounds the image. The frame goes beyond defining the edges of the image; it helps with the visual storytelling by guiding perception and adding depth to a complex view.

Framing in maximalist photography isn't about neatly isolating your subject so it stands alone. It's about using the environment – its geometry, architecture, nature or other objects and elements – to heighten the sense of abundance that is already present in your image.[2]

Colour and texture can further enhance the impact of framing. If your environment is relatively neutral, framed subjects can pop if they contain vibrant hues. Conversely, if your background is bold and saturated, you can frame 'quieter' subjects so they don't get lost in the noise. Consider how colours in the scene contrast or harmonize, and how frames draw attention to specific areas without detracting from the abundance of the scene as a whole.

Subtle post-production editing can help to emphasize frames without overshadowing the natural energy of the scene, so consider adding slight contrast to the edges of the frame to draw attention to its content. Small adjustments to exposure, clarity or sharpness around the framed area can also guide the viewer's eye without flattening the surrounding detail. At the same time, darkening the edges very subtly or introducing a light vignette can reinforce the boundaries of the frame. However, any edits should be minor. The goal is to draw out the relationships within the complexity, ensuring that the framed subject feels intentional, but without making anything else appear secondary.

[1] *See* Organized Chaos pp. 16–17
[2] *See* Multiple Focal Points pp. 20–1

REFLECTIONS

MIRROR ELEMENTS TO EXTEND THE FRAME

Reflections add a layer of intrigue, depth and complexity to a photograph. They expand the frame, often doubling or reshaping the visible world. Rather than simply capturing what is present in front of the lens, they enable what is behind, above or beside it to be captured.

The abundance of elements in a maximalist image can risk becoming visually overwhelming, but reflections can help reorganize that abundance in creative and compelling ways. Their ability to turn an ordinary scene into a kaleidoscope of overlapping forms, colours and narratives can result in incredibly compelling and emotive images.

Reflections are especially effective when they blend seamlessly into their surroundings. They invite the viewer to engage with the familiar, alongside an additional, often hidden, layer.[1]

In this image, the still surface of the water acts as a natural mirror, perfectly duplicating the lush trees, reeds and soft gradients of the landscape above. The reflection doesn't just repeat the scene, it transforms the composition into something ethereal and dreamlike, creating a seamless symmetry that feels almost surreal.[2] There's a quiet richness here: a layered composition that combines detail, mood and balance in a single frame. The mirrored surface contributes to the visual abundance – not through excess, but through duplication – reminding us that maximalism isn't always about adding more, but about revealing what is already there.

From a technical standpoint, reflections in maximalist photography require careful framing, as the scene is already dense. The placement of a reflection can easily become chaotic or disorienting, but when used purposefully, it can add clarity, rhythm and structure to the frame. Your camera angle matters, as a slight shift in position can completely alter what is reflected and how it appears. Pay close attention to how the light interacts with reflective surfaces and how this impacts the image.[3]

During post-production, careful dodging (brightening) and burning (darkening) can help separate layers or unify them, depending on the intended effect. Colour grading can help to harmonize the real elements and their reflections, creating a unified palette between reality and reflection, or conversely, make them different for added visual contrast. Small adjustments to clarity and texture in specific areas can help soften a mirrored surface or bring it into sharp definition, but try to ensure that your changes are subtle and do not introduce unnecessary confusion or distraction.

[1] *See* Multiple Focal Points pp. 20–1
[2] *See* Symmetry pp. 28–9
[3] *See* Exaggerated Perspective pp. 30–1

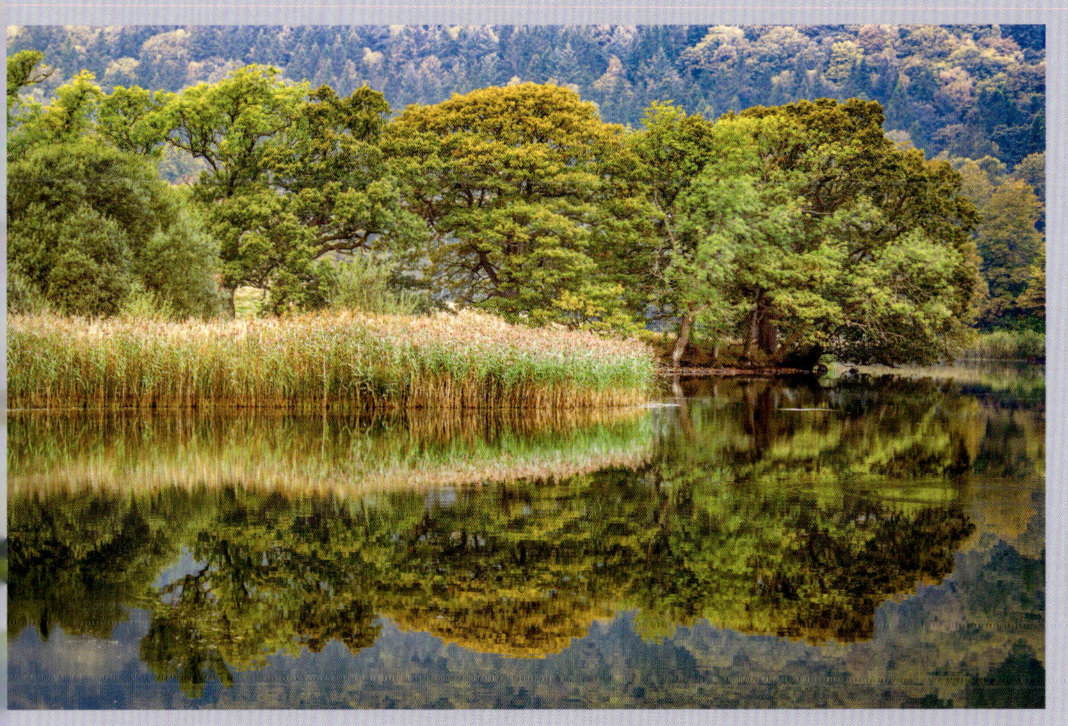

Buttermere, Antony Zacharias, 2003

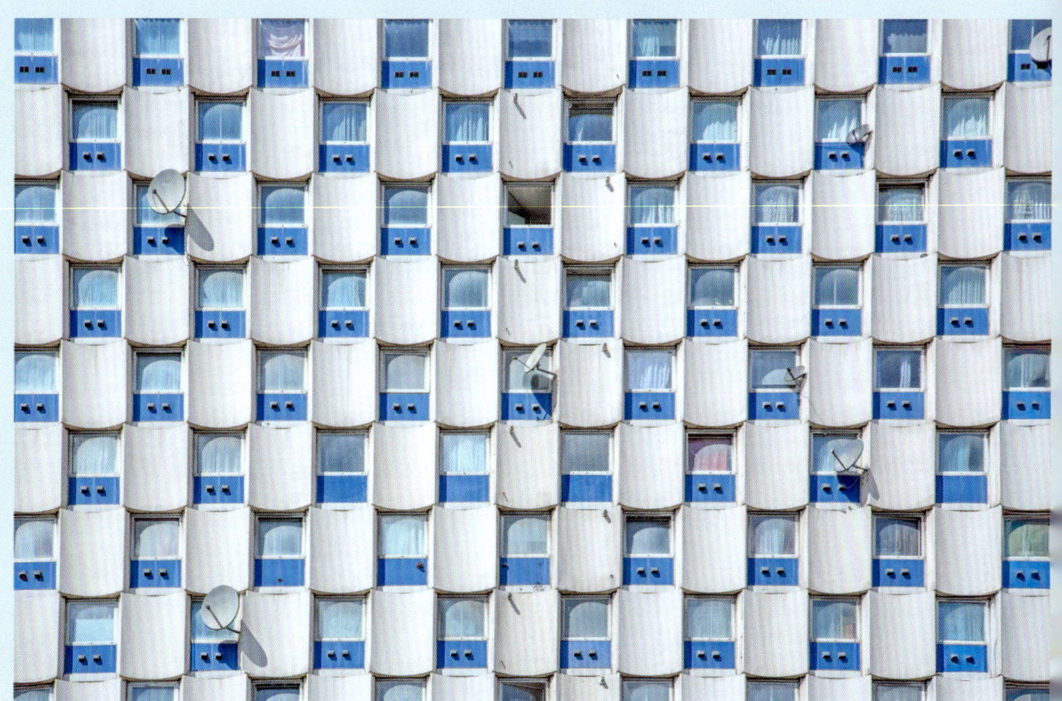

Urban Grid, Antony Zacharias, 2011

REPETITION

LAYER REPEATED FORMS FOR IMPACT

Repetition can provide structure and energy among the detail and excess in a frame. In the context of maximalism, repetition is not simple duplication – it creates momentum through recurring elements that offer a sense of cohesion. Repeating forms, colours or textures can help the viewer navigate a dense scene without feeling overwhelmed.

Viewers will find repetition interesting, as repeated elements can provide a sense of order and predictability. However, when the repetition is shifted or interrupted, it becomes dynamic. Rather than creating a sense of calm, any subtle variation will immediately stand out to an audience as they seek to interpret a shift in something seemingly uniform and predictable.

Here, the façade of a building becomes a hypnotic grid of convex white panels, highlighted by blue window frames. While each unit appears precisely repeated, on closer inspection the rhythm is broken: some windows are open, some closed, a few coloured curtains are drawn in different directions and satellite dishes and other details subtly disrupt the pattern.[1] These unexpected details create tension and focus within the apparently ordered architecture.

Although the colour palette is harmonious and soothing, the density of the pattern gives the image energy and movement. Rather than appearing clinical, the repetition feels alive, layered and engaging. The image doesn't simply depict a building, but through seemingly repetitive elements, it captures a range of subtle narrative moments embedded within the architectural structure.

Repeated forms give the eye a familiar route to follow, helping the viewer engage with each layer of the image rather than getting lost in a flood of details. This is especially helpful when you're experimenting with multiple focal points or exploring techniques that embrace complexity.[2]

When exploring repetition, be aware of your camera angle and perspective, as a slight shift in viewpoint can dramatically change how patterns line up or overlap, sometimes creating optical illusions that further enhance the maximalist feel. Conversely, introducing slight asymmetry by offsetting the repetition can spark tension and interest, making the repeated forms stand out even more.[3] Finally, if every repeated element contains a unique detail, you encourage the viewer to look closer and longer, rewarding their curiosity with new discoveries every time they scan the image.

[1] *See* Patterns pp. 24–7
[2] *See* Multiple Focal Points pp. 20–1
[3] *See* Exaggerated Perspective pp. 30–1

BREAKING THE EDGES

GO BEYOND THE BORDERS TO IMPLY MORE

Breaking the edges of a photograph is all about allowing your subject to extend beyond the boundaries of the frame, which creates a tension and energy that keeps the viewer's eye in motion. Deliberately allowing your subject to fall out of the frame encourages the viewer to think about what is happening beyond that which is visible. In a style that thrives on abundance, this technique can be especially powerful in maximalist photographs, as it amplifies the sense that your image is part of a larger, more crowded environment. It transforms the frame into a dynamic moment, inviting the viewer to imagine what lies beyond the photograph's edges.

At first, it may feel counterintuitive not to include all of your subject or the scene in full, as there is a natural instinct to want to reveal everything to your audience.[1] However, in a maximalist approach, where an image is full of detail and information, this doesn't need to be confined to the four edges of the frame. By deliberately allowing elements to extend beyond the frame, you can make an image feel expansive, alive and larger than life.

In this photograph, the vibrant rollercoaster loops demand attention as they curve out of the frame. Each colourful arch extends out of sight, which not only adds a sense of energy, but also curiosity about the extent of the ride that we cannot see: it leaves us thinking about how many more loops and drops exist just beyond our view.

Allowing objects to break the edges of the frame is also a powerful way to direct attention. The human eye naturally follows lines, and when these lines run off the edge of a picture, they generate a sense of motion in a particular direction.[2] In maximalist photography, where the goal is often to create images that burst with life and movement, these incomplete edges become an invitation to the viewer's imagination. They're a reminder that there's more to explore than is being shown and that the photograph is just one fragment of a bigger story.

The key to making this technique work is intention. Simply chopping off part of your subject at random can look accidental or disjointed, so pay attention to the angles at which your lines exit the frame, the areas of negative space you leave behind and how these decisions interact with your main focal points. Subtle shifts in framing can make a large difference.[3] Post-production cropping can strengthen the effect, making the edges feel intentional. This technique is as much about what you leave out, as what you choose to include.

[1] *See* Framing pp. 66–7
[2] *See* Leading Lines pp. 18–19
[3] *See* Exaggerated Perspectives pp. 30–1

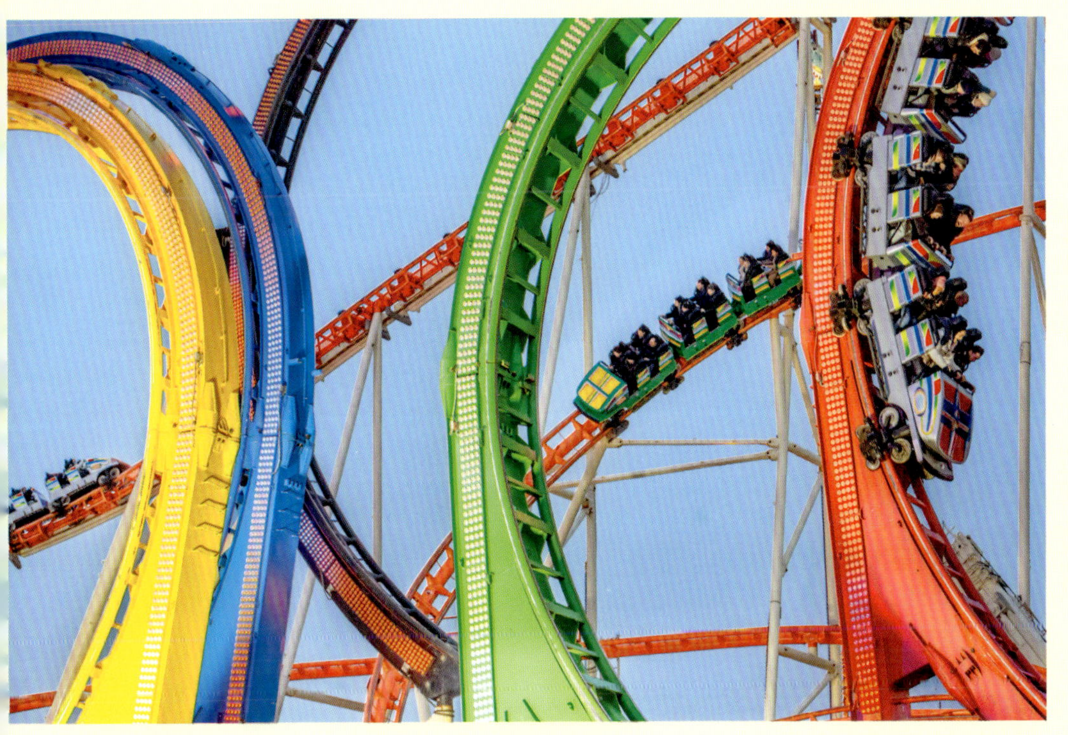

Trackwork, Antony Zacharias, 2023

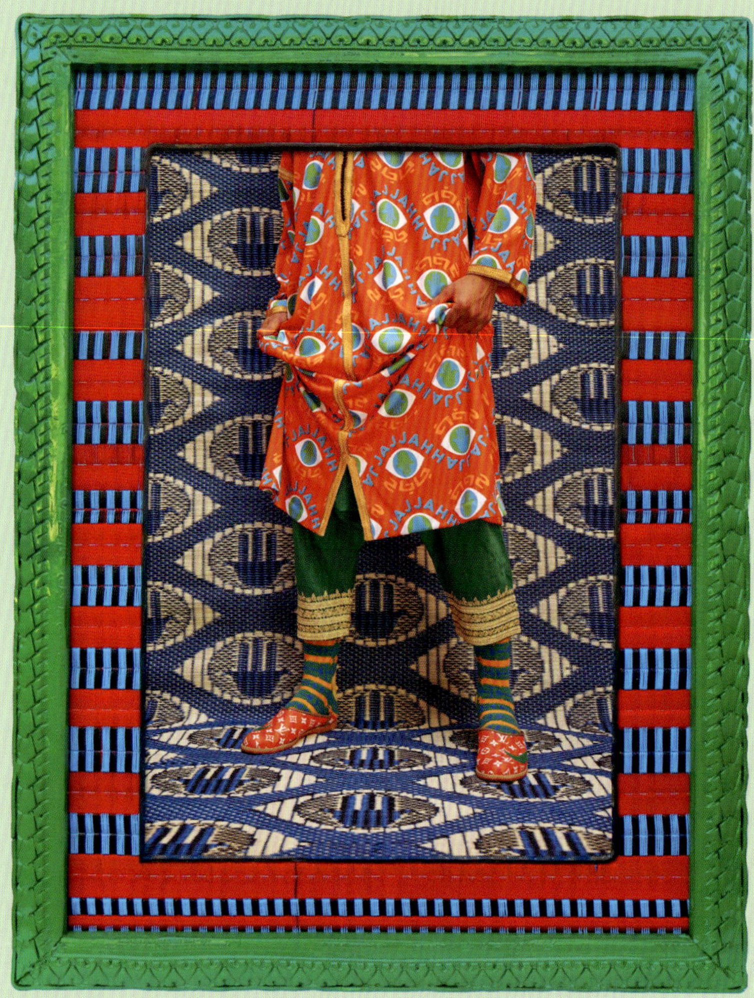

Ahmed Legs, from the *Legs* series, Hassan Hajjaj, 2022/1443

TEXTURE

HIGHLIGHT SURFACE DETAIL

Hassan Hajjaj's portrait demonstrates how textures can be interwoven to enrich a maximalist photograph. Every surface adds a distinct quality to the composition. The subject is centrally placed, yet cropped at the shoulders, wearing a vibrant orange robe covered with bold graphic motifs that both echo and clash with the geometric designs behind them. Striped socks, embroidered trousers and patterned shoes add further layers of texture that create a visual rhythm throughout. By not revealing the face of the subject, the portrait intensifies the viewer's focus on the patterns and textures, amplifying the sense of abundance.[1]

Rather than overwhelming the image, the patterns, textures and details enhance its visual weight: the portrait feels loud and complex, yet simultaneously balanced and compelling. This balance is achieved through careful composition and repetition, which helps unify the elements and guide the eye through the frame.[2]

Textures can be a powerful way to transform a busy composition into a sensory experience. By giving the viewer a sense of how surfaces might feel, you invite them to 'feel' the scene more deeply. Each texture contributes its own distinct visual and emotional tone to the photograph. Rough surfaces, for example, might evoke feelings of discomfort and harshness, while smooth textures might suggest serenity and softness. The combination of these contrasting sensations adds emotional depth and tension to a photograph.

One of the biggest challenges when including multiple textures is maintaining a balance between abundance, excess and clarity. When everything in the frame is competing for attention, it is easy for the viewer to become lost. This is even more of a risk when multiple textures are included, as a combination of intricate designs, patterned fabrics and reflective surfaces can quickly overpower an image.

An interesting technique to consider when you are combining multiple textures is to overlap them. Stacking, interweaving or placing contrasting textures together can create a sense of depth and complexity in the frame. When different textures are included, they will often interact, amplifying their similarities and their differences.[3]

The layering of textures in a maximalist photograph does more than create visual interest – it heightens the immersive experience, making the viewer feel as though they are part of the scene and the chaos of the composition. Instead of overwhelming the frame, the textures can help unify it by creating areas that intrigue the viewer and lead the eye from one area to the next.

[1] *See* Playfulness pp. 106–9
[2] *See* Patterns pp. 24–7
[3] *See* Overlap pp. 22–3

MULTIPLE EXPOSURE

INCLUDE LAYERS TO BUILD ON COMPLEXITY

Multiple exposures are a powerful tool for creating a rich, layered and complex composition. Overlaying multiple images into a single frame can build dynamic and complex narratives that reflect the excess and sensory overload that is inherent in maximalist photography. Multiple exposures intensify the visual impact of an image through their density of information combined with a sense of motion and time.

The technique involves combining multiple frames that are taken sequentially, capturing different moments (or perspectives) of the same scene. Whether this is achieved in-camera or through post-production, elements from the different images create a composition that feels fragmented, yet at the same time, cohesive.

In this joyful and immersive image, the multiple exposures layer energy, repetition and movement in a single frame.[1] The overlapping balloons, birds and figures create a surreal sense of abundance that feels celebratory and chaotic at the same time.[2] The multiple fragments of time amplify the sensory experience and capture the rhythm and liveliness in a way that a single image could not, creating a compelling scene that is complex and detailed, yet fluid and dynamic.[3]

A major challenge in multiple exposure photography – especially when you're aiming for a maximalist result – is striking the balance between overlapping elements and chaos.[4] If you simply stack your shots without thought, the scene can easily become confused and overwhelming. Instead, consider how each new layer complements or contrasts with previous ones. Perhaps wait between each exposure to ensure that each layer introduces something fresh, or reveals different patterns of movement. The goal is to avoid visual confusion.

While multiple exposures can produce striking images, they can also tell a story about a place and the people within it. By choosing your subject and timing wisely, you can create an image full of the energy and activity that defines a particular location or event. This approach makes the image feel alive, capturing not just what happened, but how it unfolded over time.

Remember that maximalism isn't just about filling the frame: it's about using the abundance of details to create a richer narrative. To ensure the final image remains inviting rather than overwhelming, be mindful of how you arrange the various elements, both in-camera and during post-processing. Every element in a maximalist photograph should have a part to play, whether it's adding to the sense of place, movement, story or emotion.

[1] *See* Playfulness pp. 106–9

[2] *See* Surrealism pp. 102–5

[3] *See* Repetition pp. 70–1

[4] *See* Organized Chaos pp. 16–17

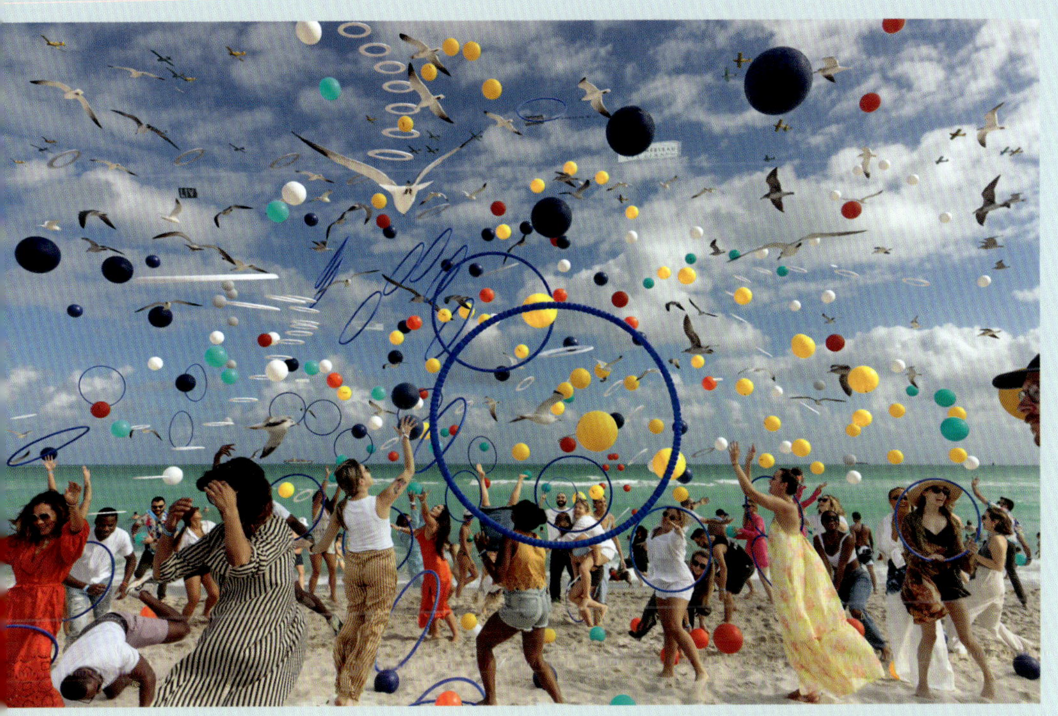

Partygoers, *Miami Beach*, Pelle Cass, 2023

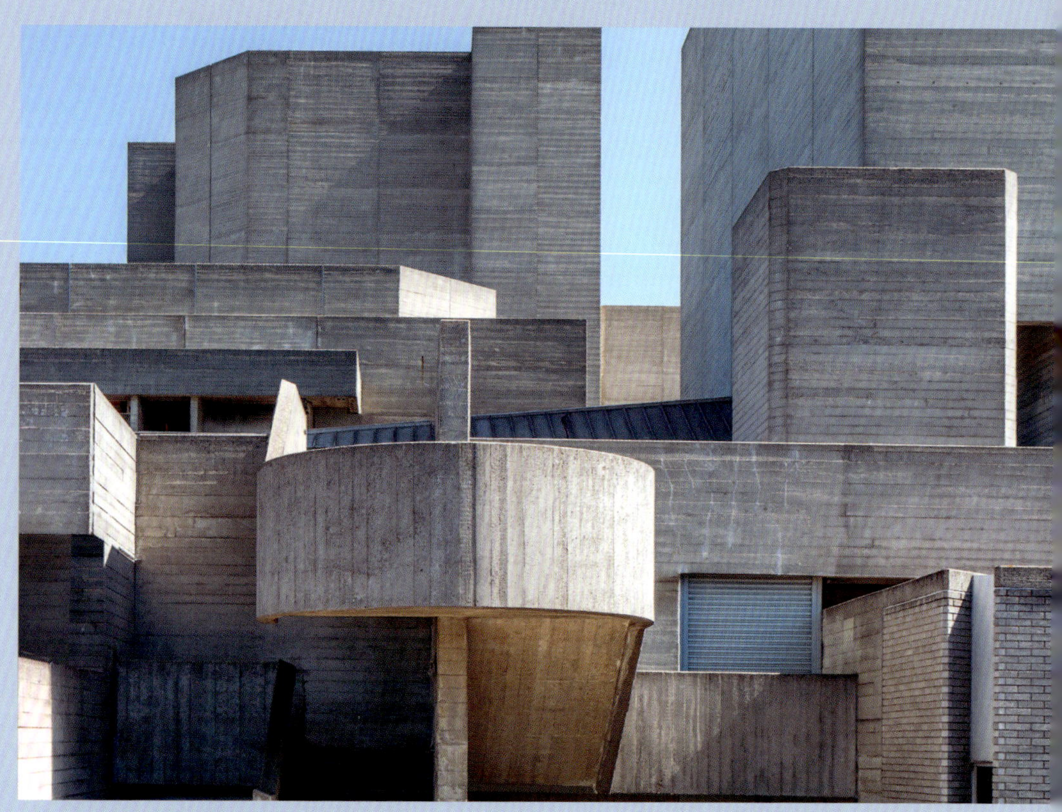

Brutalist Study XI, Antony Zacharias, 2017

SHAPE AND GEOMETRY

USE SHAPE AND FORM TO CREATE STRUCTURE

In this image, the subject initially appears as a uniform block of grey concrete, but a closer look reveals a compelling arrangement of overlapping shapes. The repeated patterns and strong geometric forms create a complex visual rhythm that immediately engages the eye. Instead of relying on colour or texture for maximalist impact, the abundance here comes from repetition and variation in shape and form. Each architectural element interacts with the others through shadow, light and lines, resulting in a scene that feels both intricate and meticulously composed.

What makes geometry so effective in a maximalist context is its ability to organize visual complexity without reducing it.[1] Incorporating it into maximalist photographs is about more than just arranging shapes in a scene: it is a way to bring structure and visual flow to images that are full of content. Shapes and lines can act like anchor points, making sure that the elements in the frame feel connected, rather than layered randomly on top of one another. By actively searching for circles, squares, triangles and more organic forms in your environment, you will start to notice how they naturally guide the eye.[2]

No matter your subject or scene, there is a universal language in shape and form that can help tie the content together in a maximalist frame. The beauty of incorporating geometry into your work is that it works regardless of the subject matter, helping to arrange details into patterns that feel intentional and satisfying.[3]

When you're out shooting, observe how shape and form appear in unexpected places. The key is to let these forms speak for themselves, guiding your eye naturally from one part of the image to another. Look at how different shapes connect or divide your composition, and rather than relying on strict, predetermined rules, focus on how the different elements interact – how a soft, curving line might intersect with a sharper edge, for example. Repeating shapes can create a sense of rhythm that invites the audience to linger. You want to maintain a sense of abundance, letting your scene overflow with interesting elements, but still give your viewer some kind of path to follow. Subtle post-production adjustments can help draw attention to these elements without detracting from the overall abundance of the scene.

[1] *See* Organized Chaos pp. 16–17
[2] *See* Multiple Focal Points pp. 20–1
[3] *See* Patterns pp. 24–7

MAGNIFY THE CHAOS

The ability to zoom up close to magnify a subject and reveal a vivid, complex composition full of depth can create an incredibly compelling image. These close-up views of textures, patterns and colours reveal more than a mere glimpse of a subject; they show the beauty that can be found hidden in the smallest details. What can be viewed as perhaps mundane from a distance can be transformed into something astonishing when viewed closely.[1]

Unlike traditional macro photographs that often isolate a subject, a maximalist macro image should fill the frame with vibrant patterns, intricate structures and a density of visual information. These images naturally invite exploration and intrigue: as a viewer spends more time investigating the scene, so more complex and interesting elements will be discovered.[2]

Although the frame may be densely filled with elements, it is still important to ensure there is a natural flow and harmony. With so much complexity it can be easy to overwhelm the viewer, so it is essential to arrange or select your elements thoughtfully. A well-considered composition requires thought about structure and order. It should feel as though every element contributes to the image, rather than creating visual confusion – there is a fine balance between capturing abundance without it becoming too chaotic.

Colour and light are important factors that will influence how the audience views your image. Bright or intense colours can amplify the content and give a feeling of visual richness, while the lighting will determine how details and textures are revealed – lighting from the side will emphasize textures, for example, while frontal lighting will flatten them. Sharpness is another consideration in this type of image, and it is essential that the camera doesn't move at all during the exposure; a tripod and remote release or timer are essential. As the depth of field will be very small at close focusing distances, a small aperture or layer-stacking may be needed to keep more of the scene in focus.

This image captures part of a naturally formed geode, revealing a beautiful array of intricate patterns and textures that appear extraordinary at such proximity. The beauty and complexity of the crystal structures are captivating, and close-up it appears almost abstract.[3] There is an abundance of visual information in the frame – colour, shape, texture and form – rewarding the viewer with new discoveries at every glance.[4]

[1] *See* Framing pp. 66–7
[2] *See* Patterns pp. 24–7
[3] *See* Abstracts pp. 82–3
[4] *See* Beauty in Chaos pp. 86–9

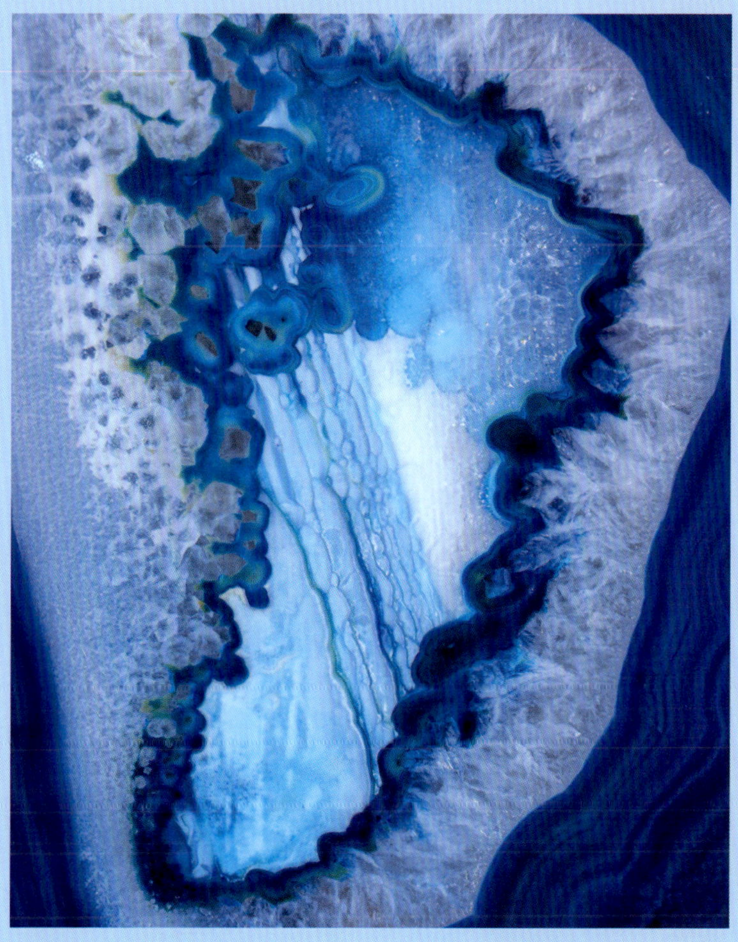

Crystalline, Antony Zacharias, 2012

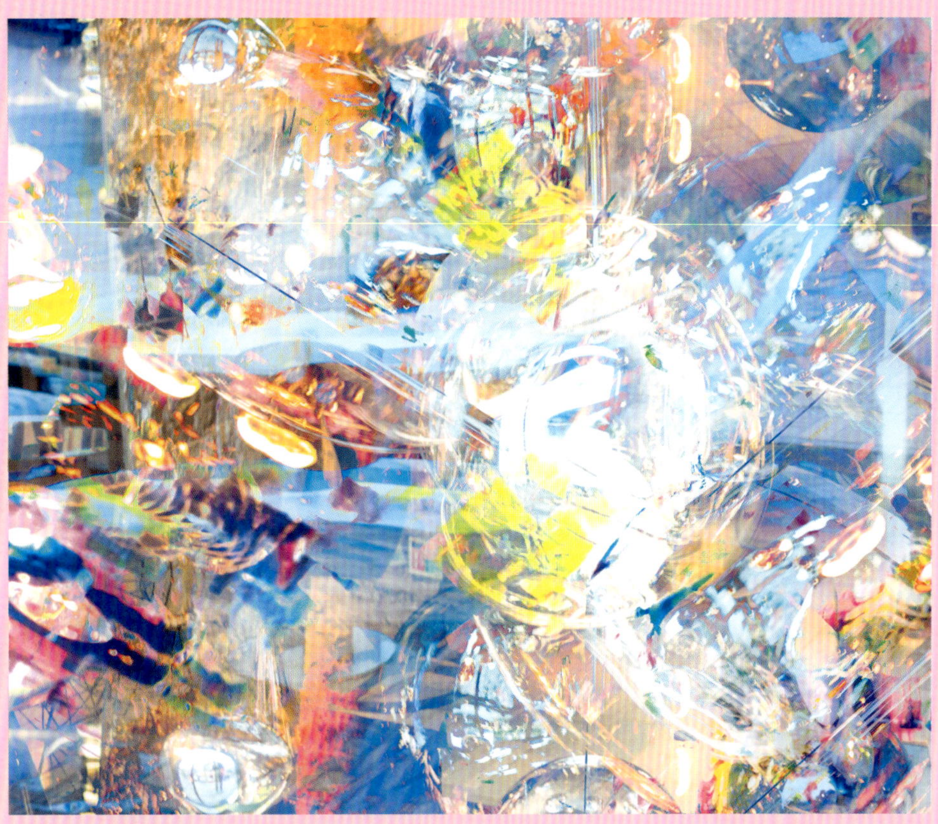

Iridescence, Antony Zacharias, 2007

DISTORT DETAIL TO BUILD INTENSITY

Abstract photography presents an endless playground where texture, shape, colour and movement can combine into something unexpected or unpredictable. Abstract images – those that don't necessarily depict a recognizable subject – can engage viewers on a deeper, more emotional level, encouraging personal exploration and interpretation. When combined with a maximalist abundance of detail, they can fully immerse the viewer, inviting them to linger, interpret and appreciate the richness and complexity of what they see.[1]

Initially, an abstract maximalist image can seem almost chaotic, so the challenge is to create an image that captivates the viewer rather than distracting them. Think about how each element benefits the photograph – how each colour, texture or swirl of light directs the audience in a certain way or serves a particular purpose.

In this photograph, you can see how the interplay of elements can become almost hypnotic. There's not a clearly defined subject to anchor the viewer's gaze; instead, the image is a combination of iridescent hues and reflective surfaces. Shapes and forms overlap and blend, creating an effect that changes depending on where you focus your attention.

When creating this type of image, it helps to look for sources of texture and colour that already have a sense of fluidity. It might be refracted light shining through glass, a reflection or the swirling patterns in a macro shot. Consider your framing and how each element will contribute to the overall sense of depth and energy. Think about the interplay of different colours: do they complement or clash in a way that feels exciting or emotive? Pay attention to how highlights and shadows create dimensionality, even when there's no obvious subject. Rather than worrying about whether the viewer can identify what they're looking at, focus on evoking an emotional response instead. Abstract imagery thrives on the tension that is created between recognition and mystery.

One of the most rewarding aspects of this approach is its ability to evoke a variety of reactions. When the subject isn't clearly defined, each viewer brings their own experiences and memories to it, interpreting shapes and colours in uniquely personal ways. The absence of a literal subject invites them to step closer, to look deeper and to let their imagination wander.[2]

[1] *See* Beauty in Chaos pp. 86–9
[2] *See* Layered Meanings pp. 134–5

STORYTELLING

BEAUTY IN CHAOS

REVEAL ORDER THROUGH OBSERVATION

At first glance, *Industrial Form* may seem like the antithesis of beauty and harmony – an overwhelming chaos of meandering industrial shapes and textures. However, in maximalist photography this kind of visual overload becomes an interesting setting for uncovering unexpected aesthetics. The dense layering of pipes, towers, tanks and scaffolding creates a chaotic rhythm that mimics nature in its complexity and interconnection. The sheer mass of detail pulls the eye in every direction, but within the disorder lies structure, repetition and form – a symmetry arising from a purpose-driven design. By framing the industrial structure, the image forces us to reconsider the boundaries of beauty, and challenges our perception of what constitutes an appealing visual landscape.[1]

There is an inherent beauty that can be found in a maximalist photograph. This is not simply by overwhelming the frame and the viewer with a barrage of information and detail, but through the unpredictable harmony, interest and intrigue that will emerge naturally through scenes of visual complexity. This notion of 'shaping complexity' acknowledges the aesthetic of the disorder itself – how a composition can resonate emotionally and visually because it feels natural and unstructured, yet at the same time harmonious and balanced.

Harmony often emerges from the unexpected alignment of seemingly random elements. What may appear chaotic at first can actually draw viewers in, inviting them to discover the subtle rhythms and relationships in a scene. This can create a sense of tension within the apparent disorder, which transforms the photograph into a complex, layered composition full of depth and visual interest.

When approaching seemingly overloaded scenes, there is a benefit to slowing down and looking beyond the excess and complexity. Taking the time to observe can result in a composition that captures the essence of the chaos infused with the beauty of the context or environment.

An effective use of colour can help to enhance the sense of chaotic beauty. Rich palettes of diverse hues can lead to vibrant scenes of harmony; when multiple colours are found together naturally, each colour interacts and contrasts with the others, resulting in an exciting scene.

[1] *See* Excess pp. 12–13

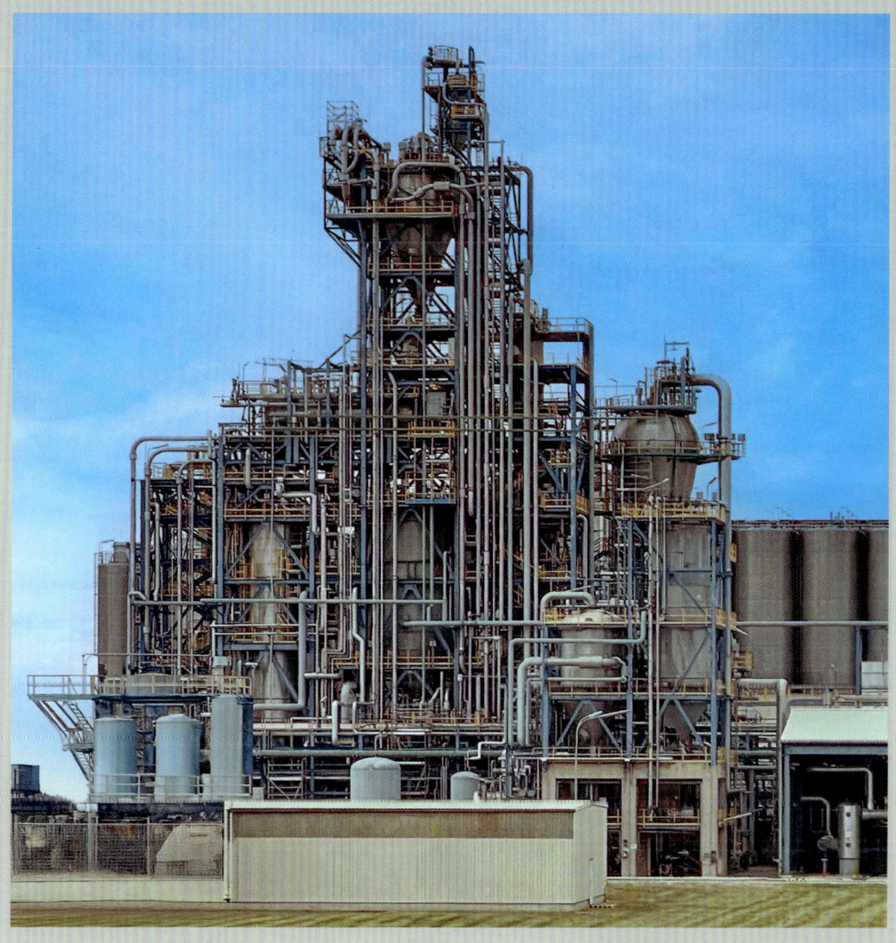

Industrial Form, Antony Zacharias, 2023

BEAUTY IN CHAOS

Bas Meeuws's image reveals how chaotic beauty can be carefully constructed in a maximalist photograph. The dense array of flowers in a vase may appear random and scattered, but every bloom is arranged deliberately. There may seem to be little structure or order, but the rich variety of colours, shapes and textures creates a natural sense of balance and visual rhythm. Each flower stands out on its own, yet together they form a composition that is both joyful and calming. Despite the apparent chaos, the image feels serene rather than overwhelming. Its layered richness invites the viewer to pause and explore, discovering small details and subtle relationships that transform the scene into an engaging and unexpectedly harmonious experience.[2]

Considered control of lighting and exposure helps ensure that chaotic scenes remain engaging. Often, softer diffused lighting will complement these settings, helping to reveal intricate details and subtle colour graduations without becoming too distracting. Directional lighting can also help accentuate textures and patterns, which can result in visually compelling images. In post-production, small adjustments to vibrance, contrast and clarity can further enhance the natural harmony of the elements.

Images of complexity and excess can result in a flood of visual information, with each element competing for attention in the frame. Yet, it is the ability to find and highlight beauty within the disorder that makes these images emotionally powerful and deeply resonant. This is one of the most striking qualities of maximalist photography – its ability to express powerful emotion through visual excess. The dense layering of elements can evoke a wide range of feelings, from excitement and wonder to tension or unease, depending how they are arranged together.

The beauty of this chaos lies not only in its emotional impact, but in how those feelings are communicated visually. The balance might not be immediately obvious but may become so on closer inspection: in the way colours interact, how forms appear together, repetition or how visual weight is distributed across the frame. In this way, maximalist photography becomes a space for visual and emotional exploration that encourages the viewer to spend time, to notice, to feel and to connect.

[2] *See* Quiet Moments pp. 90–3

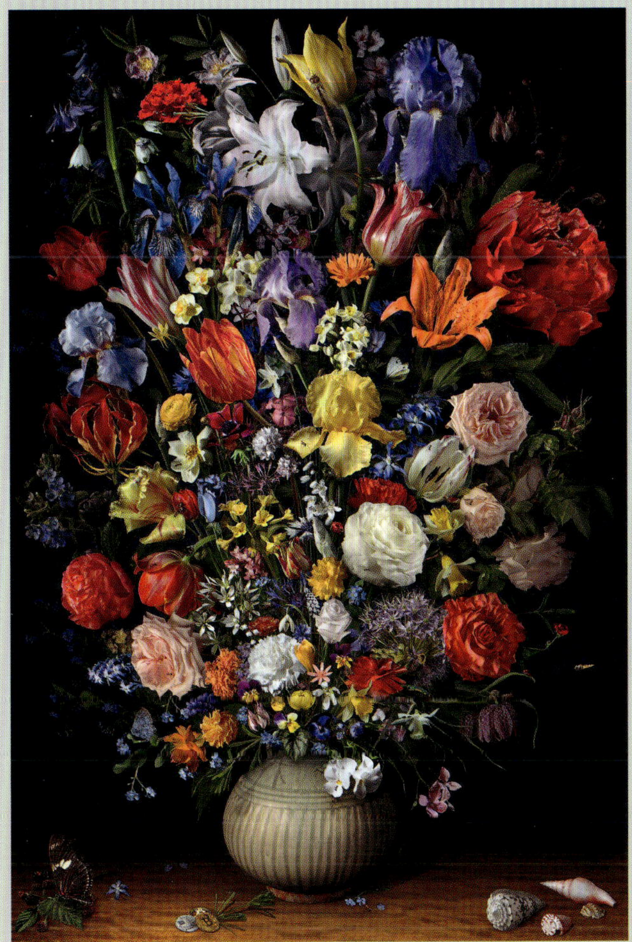

Untitled (#205), after Jan Brueghel the Elder, Bas Meeuws, 2024

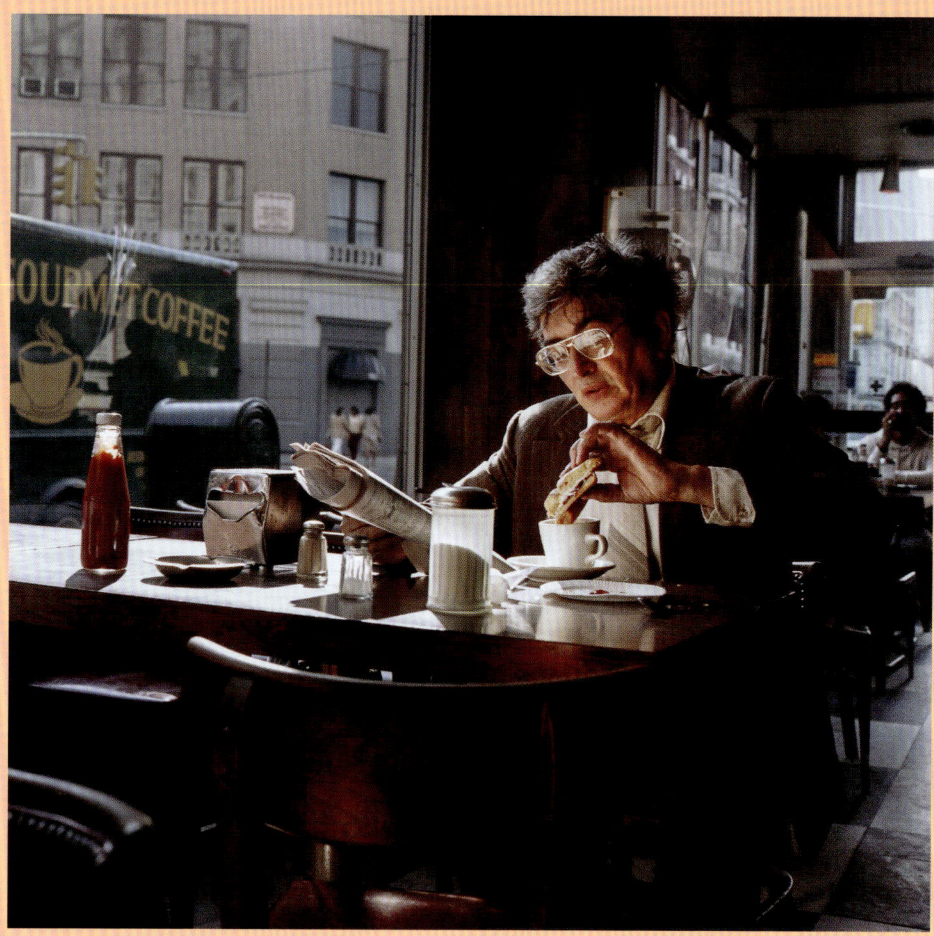

Coffee and a Sandwich, Janet Delaney, 1985

QUIET MOMENTS

LOOK FOR SPACE WITHIN THE NOISE

The notion of quiet moments in maximalist photography might seem counterintuitive at first: surely a style that is defined by layers of excess, abundance and complexity would leave little room for feelings of gentleness, calm or introspection? Yet, this assumption overlooks the subtlety of how quiet can emerge not in spite of visual abundance, but because of it.

Stripping away the visual information is not what is required for the 'quiet' in a maximalist photograph. It is about considered compositions that create an overall sense of peace or solitude among the complexity of a scene. Rather than reducing visual elements to find a calm space, maximalist photography embraces complexity while encouraging us to look more carefully. It is about placing attention deliberately, about choosing a focal point that infers softness among the rich surrounding details.

The key lies in how the details are arranged and how they relate to a moment that feels emotionally still or thoughtful. When composed with care, a frame filled with information can provide an unexpected sense of peace. Achieving this balance starts with identifying a subject or moment that has the potential to be tranquil, despite being surrounded by a chaotic environment. This quiet may come from a subtle beauty found in an overlooked moment, or from the emotional atmosphere in a scene. In either case, the goal is not to reduce the visual information but to allow it to support the essence of the frame.

In *Coffee and a Sandwich*, Janet Delaney's maximalism takes on a quiet and introspective form, unfolding within the seemingly ordinary moment of a person eating alone in a café. The image is layered with visual detail – signs, a cluttered table, newspapers, reflections in the window and glimpses of the city beyond – which all contribute to a dense, textured composition. Yet despite this abundance, none of these details dominates the frame. Instead, they all support a moment of a quiet human routine, and the scene feels calm despite the cluttered environment. This image reminds us that maximalism doesn't have to be loud or vibrant to demand attention – it can be a quiet, observant moment that emerges within a visually complex scene.

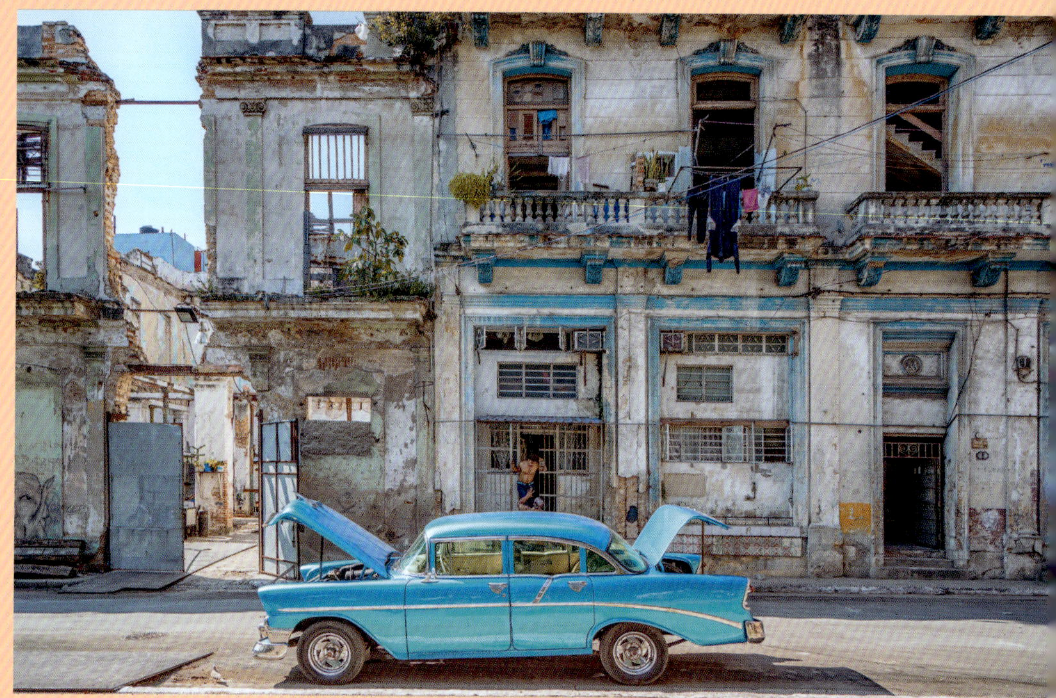

In Need of Repair, Antony Zacharias, 2016

A similar dynamic unfolds in *In Need of Repair*. Here, an old building stands in a state of disrepair with a classic car parked out front. The building's peeling paint, cracked walls and faded teal accents tell a story of time and wear. In contrast, the car is shiny and well-kept, with its door and bonnet open suggesting ongoing life and maintenance. Despite the implied action, the scene is quiet and the moment feels paused.[1] The occupant or mechanic is visible in the background, but there is no urgency; they aren't frantically repairing anything, but seem absorbed in their task at a leisurely pace. In this way, their presence helps anchor the calm.

Patience plays a critical role in composing photographs such as these. Quiet maximalist images are rarely staged and are found through observation and a willingness to wait. You need to be aware of what may become visually interesting or emotionally resonant, but also open to the unexpected and any factors that create a feeling of serenity.

Editing can refine the sense of quiet without muting the overall vibrancy. Subtle adjustments – reducing contrast around busy areas or a subtle boost in exposure or warmth, for example – can bring out the soft glow around the subject, which can help reinforce the quiet mood without diminishing the scene's integrity.

[1] *See* Energy in Stillness pp. 136–7

WONDER AND DELIGHT

CREATE A FRAME TO INSPIRE JOY

In maximalist photography, wonder and delight can emerge so strongly from visually rich and compelling scenes that they captivate the viewer and spark a sense of amazement and excitement. Rather than having a single, striking focal point, these images are filled with an array of dynamic and dazzling elements.[1]

That said, it isn't about merely filling the picture with an abundance of disconnected content. Wonder arises either when the familiar becomes extraordinary, or through the revelation of something the viewer doesn't ordinarily get to see.[2] However, composition is crucial in preventing the excitement from becoming chaotic. Maximalist images still require intentional structure: strong leading lines or sweeping curves that can guide the eye through the scene in a deliberate journey, or a repeating pattern or spiral of colour to keep the viewer engaged. By incorporating these compositional anchors, the energy of the image will remain focused, allowing each amazing detail to shine without overwhelming the frame.[3]

Colour is often a driving force in creating this sense of wonder. Bold hues can ignite an immediate spark of excitement. However, the arrangement of these colours matters just as much as their intensity: their positioning can guide the viewer's eye through the scene, ensuring they experience a flow of surprises rather than confusing chaos.

In Cath Simard's image, *Eurêka*, the fluorescent green hues of the aurora borealis illuminate the serenity of the mountain range. The colourful reflections revealed on the wet sand adds an air of mystery to the scene. These natural wonders are awe-inspiring, and the sheer range of visual contrasts makes the image dynamic and compelling. From the sharp outlines of the mountains to the soft blur of the flowing water, a multitude of elements leads the viewer through a path of discovery. Colour amplifies feelings of amazement, which alludes to a world out of the ordinary. Rather than just conveying calm, the subdued palette heightens the emotion, suggesting this is a rare and unique event.[4]

Movement is another way of introducing excitement into a richly detailed photograph. A still image can suggest motion by capturing flowing shapes, angled lines or overlapping forms that hint at activity. These don't necessarily have to be rendered in sharp focus – a slight blur or multiple exposure can convey the buzz of the moment in an equally powerful way.

Pauline Ballet's image shifts the focus from nature's awe-inspiring landscapes to a crowd teeming with human energy. Taken from a

[1] *See* Organized Chaos pp. 16–17
[2] *See* Beauty in Chaos pp. 86–8
[3] *See* Leading Lines pp. 18–19
[4] *See* Emotive Colour pp. 48–9

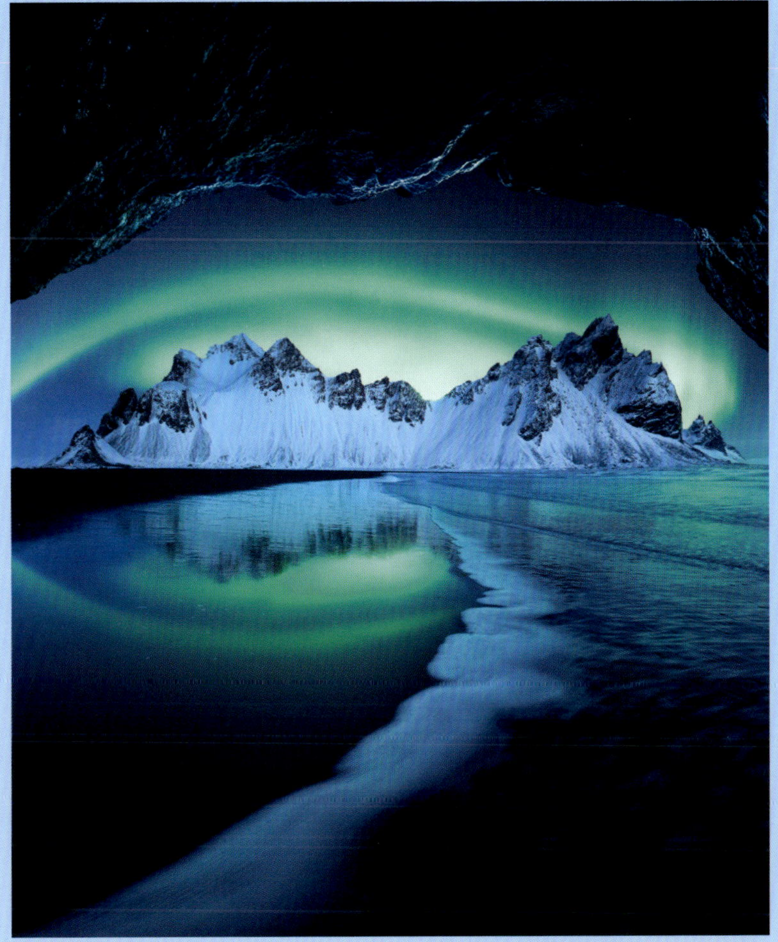

Eurêka, Cath Simard, 2020

slightly elevated vantage point, it reveals a large crowd of people extending in all directions. A central figure stands out as the main focus, but each person in the crowd represents a distinct point of interest, all in different clothing with varied expressions and poses. The resulting image is both chaotic and fascinating – a testament to the intensity of shared human experiences. In maximalist photography, such scenes thrive on the interaction between repetition and individual variation. Here, countless people are photographed gathered together, but zooming in reveals diverse connections and personal stories – moments of anticipation, admiration and excitement.

Lighting can reinforce an atmosphere of wonder or delight in an image. Harsh, direct light can create dramatic highlights and strong shadows, while a softer, more diffused glow can render the scene with a dreamlike quality.

Scale and perspective can also be used to heighten wonder within maximalist photography. When vastness is conveyed through a sweeping landscape or enormous crowd, the viewer is reminded of their own smallness. A slightly unexpected vantage point, such as a view from above, can further immerse the viewer, transforming them from a passive observer into a participant.[5]

Finally, post-production offers an opportunity to fine tune the sense of wonder. Boosting saturation, vibrance or contrast can help colours pop, while dodging and burning can highlight key textures or shapes. Slight manipulations are all that's needed to help make the image seem slightly more fantastical. Care needs to be taken to ensure this is not overdone.

[5] *See* Exaggerated Perspectives pp. 30–1

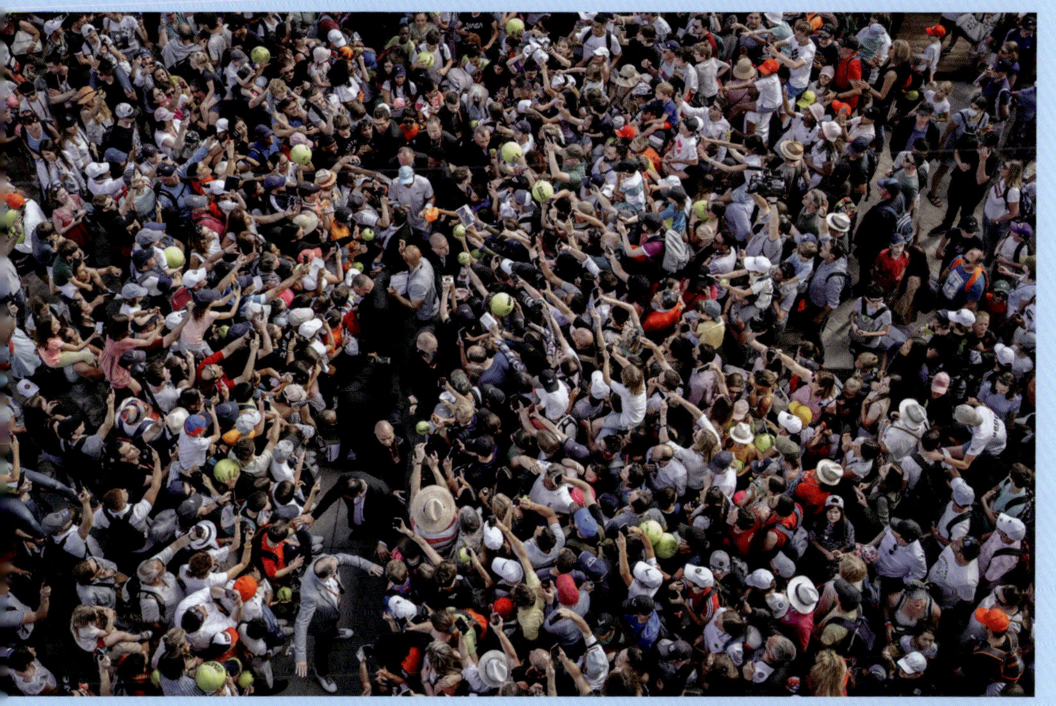

Rafael Nadal, Roland Garros, Pauline Ballet, 2022

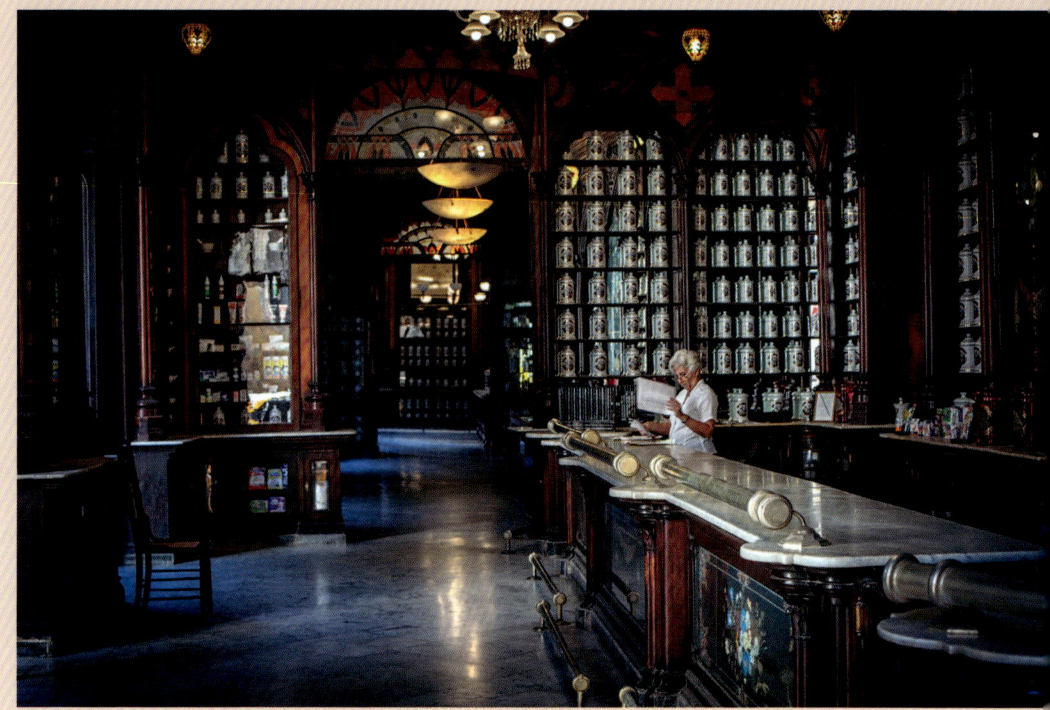

The Shopkeeper, Antony Zacharias, 2017

NOSTALGIA

USE LAYERING TO GIVE A SENSE OF THE PAST

A maximalist scene creates plenty of space for rich, emotional storytelling, as instead of isolating a single symbol of the past, there is an abundance of elements, layers of memory and remnants of history filling the frame.

Maximalist compositions are often packed with visual clues that collectively speak to time passing, to things left behind or moments remembered. They deepen the emotional tone, allowing the viewer to become immersed in the feeling, rather than simply observing it. The photograph becomes a kind of time capsule, allowing the audience to sense a presence that has passed, or a moment that's slipping away. It invites a more personal engagement from the viewer, where each person brings their own memories, experiences and associations to the image, projecting their own stories onto the scene.

One way to achieve this atmosphere is through the careful curation of the frame. The positioning of objects, patterns and other details needs to be thoughtfully considered, as these are the elements that will draw each viewer into the image in a unique and impactful way.

Light and colour play a critical role in shaping the nostalgic narrative in an image. Soft, diffused lighting – whether natural or artificial – will enhance the emotional presence of objects and subjects, while stronger contrasts can enhance a sense of longing, where some details appear sharp and clear and others fade into darkness. Faded or muted hues naturally evoke a sense of the past.

A human presence, whether direct or implied, will always intensify the emotional resonance of a scene. The image presented here makes us feel as if we are stepping back in time, with the intricate woodwork, towering shelves and soft glow of the lighting contributing to a richly nostalgic atmosphere. However, it is the lone woman behind the counter who brings the image to life. Absorbed in her task, her presence doesn't demand attention, yet she becomes the emotional anchor for the scene, providing the composition with a sense of lived experience.[1]

Texture and decay also contribute significantly to the melancholic feel of an image. The presence of cracks, peeling paint or rust will suggest the slow passing of time. Layering such textures can create a tactile feeling for the viewer – a sense of history that can almost be felt as well as seen. In this image, for example, every corner of the frame is filled with textures and details, from the marble countertops to the ornate fixtures. Each of these elements invites the viewer to investigate a scene drenched with the sense of a time gently receding into the past.

[1] *See* Quiet Moments pp. 90–3

VULNERABILITY

HIGHLIGHT THE FRAGILITY BENEATH THE EXCESS

In this image, Christy Lee Rogers captures the essence of vulnerability through an abstract and maximalist lens. A swirl of bodies, fabrics and motion blur together in a scene that is filled with colour, resulting in a dreamlike composition that feels weightless, yet full of intensity. The figures are partially obscured by the floating fabrics that both hide and reveal their presence. Rather than isolating the subject, the maximalist approach heightens the intensity of emotion – the layering of textures and movement reflects the layered nature of vulnerability itself, creating something complex, sensitive and personal.[1]

Vulnerability in maximalist photography uses visual abundance to highlight emotional depth rather than hide it. When a scene is full of colour, texture and overlapping forms, a quiet sign or expression can stand out even more clearly. Instead of distracting from the subject, the detailed environment draws attention to them, making their openness and fragility feel all the more powerful. The contrast between the emotional tone of the subject and the energy of the scene creates a strong connection with the viewer.

Composition will inevitably play a pivotal role in reinforcing feelings of vulnerability. Central placement of the subject surrounded by other objects or people will create a strong image. Alternatively, situating them slightly off-centre can convey a sense of displacement, as if they're unsure how they fit into the larger scene. The challenge is to ensure that the environment feels genuinely full without smothering the emotional focal point. Every element or shape should serve a purpose, either by reinforcing the theme or by framing the subject in a meaningful way.

Your lighting choices can enhance the emotion in an image. Soft, diffused light creates a gentle, thoughtful mood, while stronger, directional light can reveal raw vulnerability by highlighting sharp contrasts and adding drama to the scene.

Colour choices are an equally important consideration. In this image, the rich saturated colours of the clothing takes on a bright fluid quality that enhances the emotional tone. These colours drift and merge, gently creating a softness that supports the mood of vulnerability.[2]

Texture plays a key role too, as the delicate folds in the fabric catch the underwater light, suggesting both the softness of the material and the emotional sensitivity of the figures. In a maximalist context, these details help to express vulnerability with depth and subtlety.[3]

[1] *See* Long Exposure pp. 44–5
[2] *See* Emotive Colour pp. 48–9
[3] *See* Textures pp. 74–5

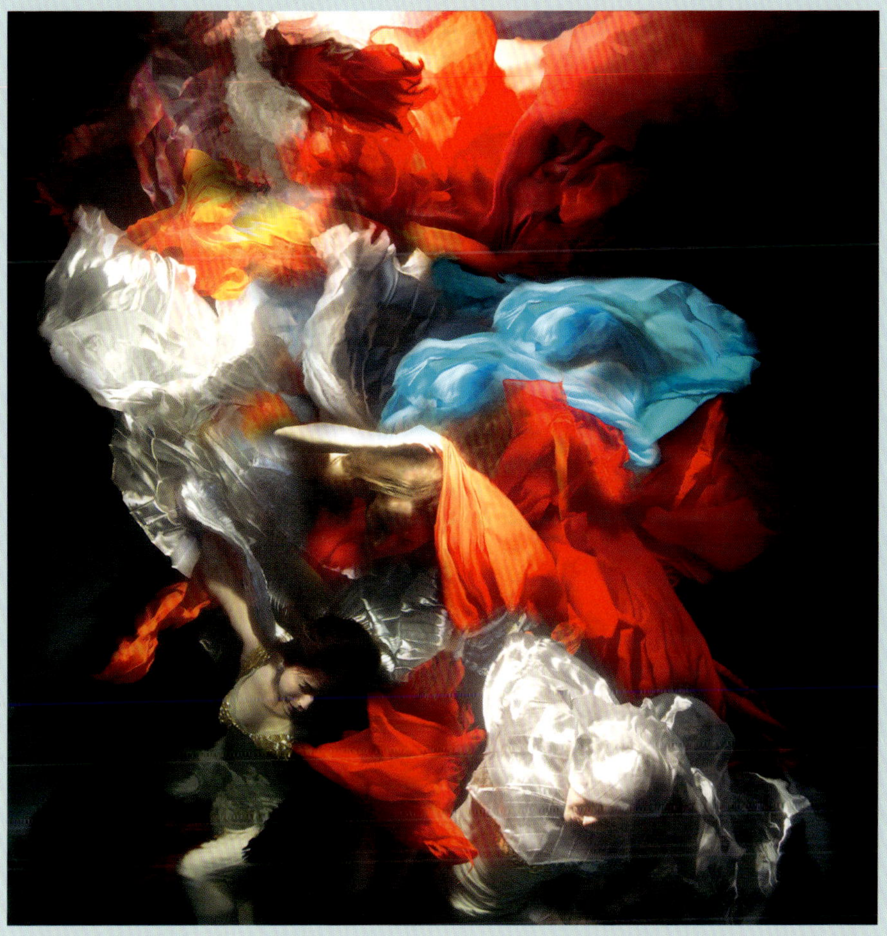

Riders of the Light, Christy Lee Rogers, 2020

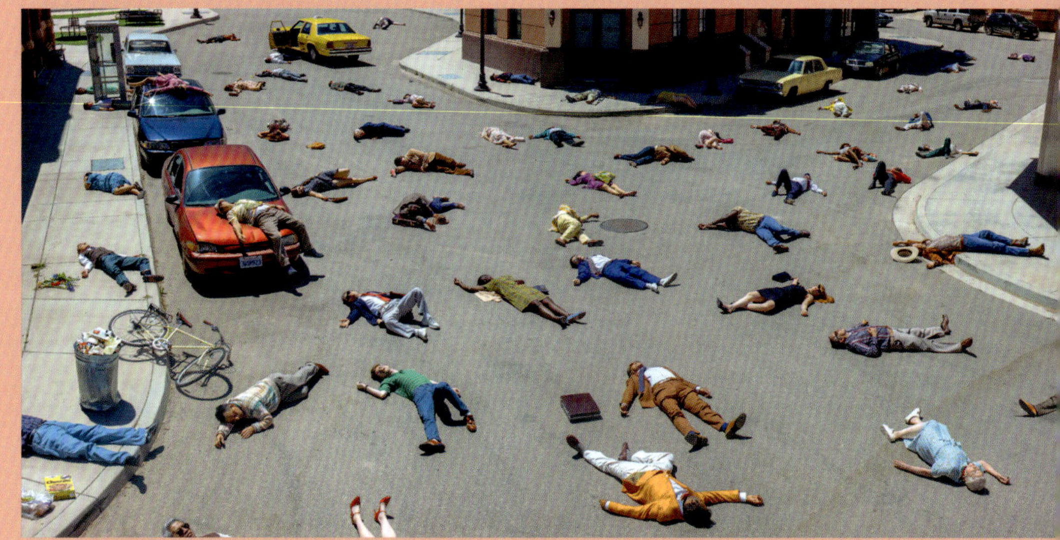

Sleep, Alex Prager, 2022

SURREALISM

PLAY WITH COMPLEX REALITIES

Surrealism in maximalist photography is not simply about creating strange, dreamlike or conceptual images – it is about using exaggeration and excess to challenge our usual sense of reality. Rather than presenting a single surreal moment, these images offer layers of unusual and wonderful details, creating scenes where reality feels stretched, tilted or reimagined. The viewer is invited on a journey that feels unpredictable, yet oddly grounded through elements they recognize.

In this context, surrealism isn't defined by unfamiliar objects, but by familiar ones used in unfamiliar ways. The surreal is amplified in a maximalist context with abundance and exaggerated visual elements such as scale, repetition and visual density. Where everyday objects appear in unnatural numbers or arrangements, or time feels suspended or irrelevant, this will disrupt the viewer's sense of 'normal', while simultaneously offering a deep and immersive experience. Maximalism enhances surrealism by making the unreal feel both physical and tangible, with the resulting image becoming both visually dense and emotionally charged.

This abundance is a key element in surreal maximalist imagery: where instead of one object appearing out of place, the frame might contain many. Alex Prager's compelling image depicts dozens of people lying motionless across a city street. The scene is intensely staged, with every figure and object positioned carefully. The resulting surreal effect comes not from a single strange detail, but from the sheer scale of the repetition. Why are these people all lying down? What moment are we witnessing? The street is familiar; the cars and buildings are ordinary, yet the human behaviour is entirely disconnected from our everyday reality. This tension between a mundane environment and abnormal activity creates a strong surreal feeling.

There is a hypnotic, pattern-like quality created by the number of bodies filling the scene. They are spaced out evenly, but not symmetrically, which creates a rhythm that feels both intentional and disorienting. There is no obvious story or cause, no visible distress or explanation, only the eerie stillness of so many people behaving identically in a context that is extraordinary. This is where maximalist surrealism excels: it draws you in as you ask more questions, without providing answers or a clear resolution. This makes the image feel like a frozen dream or suspended reality.

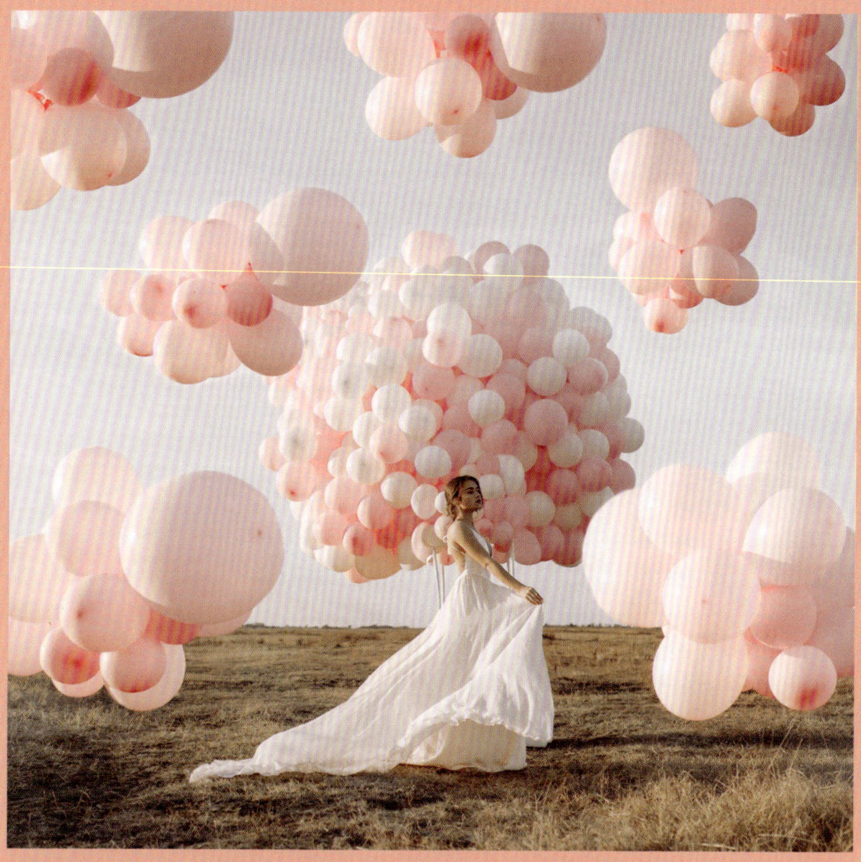

Balloon Paradise, Jovana Rikalo, 2018

In contrast, Jovana Rikalo's image explores surreal maximalism through softness and fantasy rather than unease. A woman in a flowing white dress stands in a wide, open landscape, surrounded by clusters of pale pink balloons suspended in the space. Although dreamlike, the scene is rendered with clarity, and its surreal quality emerges due to scale and the distorted reality. Balloons this large and this numerous do not behave this way in reality; they appear too light to be hovering and too many to be explained.

The contrast between the stark natural ground and the artificial, dreamlike presence of the balloons creates a surreal contradiction in this photograph. The woman, centrally placed, becomes both anchor and subject within this imagined atmosphere. Her dress echoes the softness of the balloons, blending her into the scene, while also establishing her as the focal point. This image doesn't shock – its surrealism is built on beauty and lightness. The maximalist context of hundreds of balloons all carefully arranged makes the fantasy feel fully realized rather than merely suggested.

To create a strong surrealist image through maximalism, it is important to control the scale and detail in the scene. Forced perspective or unique angles can help you manipulate scale and enhance the surreal effects.[1] Lighting, colour, textures, patterns and repetition are also powerful tools for disrupting what we perceive as 'normal'.

Surrealism ultimately invites the viewer to question the nature of reality, and planning is usually essential. The surreal only becomes effective when its visual contradictions are embedded in an otherwise believable world. How the elements are placed in the frame is hugely important, as surreal maximalist images are often strongest when every element feels as though it has been positioned deliberately.[2]

Think about the emotional tone of your scene and the feelings you want to convey, be it unease, wonder, humour, excitement or something else altogether. Whatever you choose, build the surrealist composition towards that emotional goal. It is important to remember that the most powerful surreal images are not chaotic or unnecessarily cluttered, but are carefully constructed. Each element is placed to guide the viewer and invite their curiosity and wonder, encouraging them to question what they are seeing.

[1] *See* Exaggerated Perspectives pp. 30–1
[2] *See* Symbolism pp. 118–21

PLAYFULNESS

FIND FUN IN VISUAL EXCESS

In *Bouncy Ball*, Maisie Cousin's eponymous subject is awash with shimmering stars and glistening shapes, set against a colourful background of pink and purple tones. Initially, it might seem like a simple macro shot, but the explosion of sparkles, colours and textures draws you in.[1] The ball appears like a miniature world – a tiny galaxy contained in a small sphere – while the background complements the subject through its similar vibrancy. The photograph feels playful precisely because it's unapologetically bright and full of surprises. Each drop or star-shape is a small discovery, and the glossy surface of the ball reflects the surrounding colours in a kaleidoscopic manner. It's an image that invites the viewer to look closer and envision themselves as part of this imaginary, fun-filled world.

Playful maximalist photography is all about harnessing the sheer joy of visual abundance. It is about celebrating the bright, unusual, unexpected or eccentric in a way that makes the viewer feel part of what they are looking at. It goes beyond filling the frame with random or disjointed content and instead focuses on capturing the spirit of a unique, curious and seemingly spontaneous collection of elements. Playful maximalism taps into a childlike wonder full of colourful fun and humour.

One of the foundations for playful maximalism is to let go of any preconceived rules: technique and composition remain important, but the essence should be to approach your subject with a sense of fun and experimentation. Explore your subject in a way that ignites your own curiosity and allow yourself to be playful in doing so. Happy accidents are more likely to occur in this way, and a reflection, a splash of colour, a spontaneous gesture or unusual framing can help you create something magical.

A good starting point is to think about what feels joyful or quirky in the scene. Make this this centre of your composition (although not necessarily in the literal sense) and fill the frame with it. Think about your positioning and the lens that can help you, be it a macro lens for a close-up take or a wide-angle lens to fit in more of the scene.[2]

[1] *See* Explosive Colour pp. 46–7
[2] *See* Macro pp. 80–1

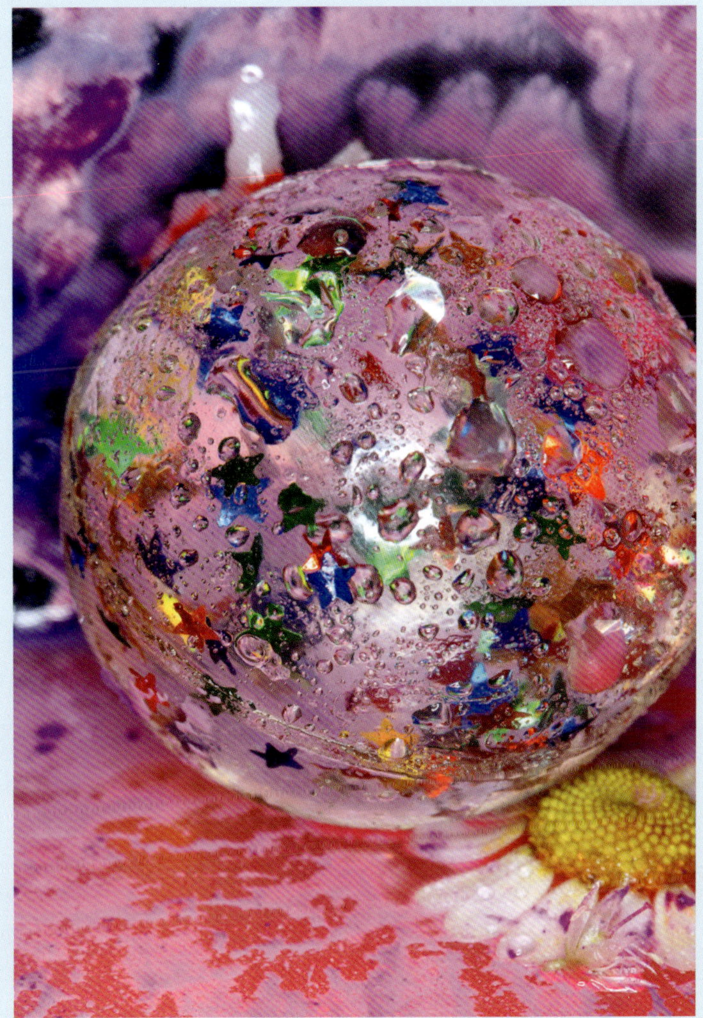

Bouncy Ball, Maisie Cousins, 2021

PLAYFULNESS

Colour and texture are important parts of a playful image, and bold, saturated tones work best. That doesn't mean you can't work with pastels or more neutral hues, but you will want to accentuate the colours in a way that feels lively. While there is no single formula for which colours to include, the key is to be intentional about how they interact. Clashing colours can be fun and energetic, while complementary tones can create a sense of harmony, even amid visual abundance.[3] Texture can add an extra dimension to your image, and a variety of textures can create a picture that is more immersive and inviting for the viewer.[4]

Lighting is another key consideration, as it can amplify or dampen the playful qualities of a maximalist scene and influence the mood. Harsh, direct lighting can add drama; brighter light will bring excitement; softer, more diffused lighting can often make a scene feel more inviting and carefree.[5]

Compositionally, playful images tend to involve breaking away from the 'classic' rules in favour of following your own creative vision. The rules don't have to be ignored completely, but first and foremost you should be thinking about how all the elements work together in the frame to set the mood of the scene and help tell your story.

Playful maximalist photography encourages storytelling through details, and there is an immediate sense of fun in Brooke DiDonato's image. Here, the figure – covered mostly in an explosion of pink, red and blue flowers – transforms the scene into something dreamlike and theatrical.[6] The flowers seem to extend beyond mere decoration, making the subject and their surroundings inseparable. This playful concealment of the subject challenges the viewer to consider the boundaries between them and their environment. The saturated colours, soft textures and deliberate visual excess turn the image into something bold, imaginative and defiantly joyful. It offers a glimpse into the photographer's sense of wonder and delight, and their ability to find humour in everyday chaos.

[3] *See* Emotive Colour pp. 48–9

[4] *See* Textures pp. 74–5

[5] *See* Dynamic Lighting pp. 40–3

[6] *See* Surrealism pp. 102–5

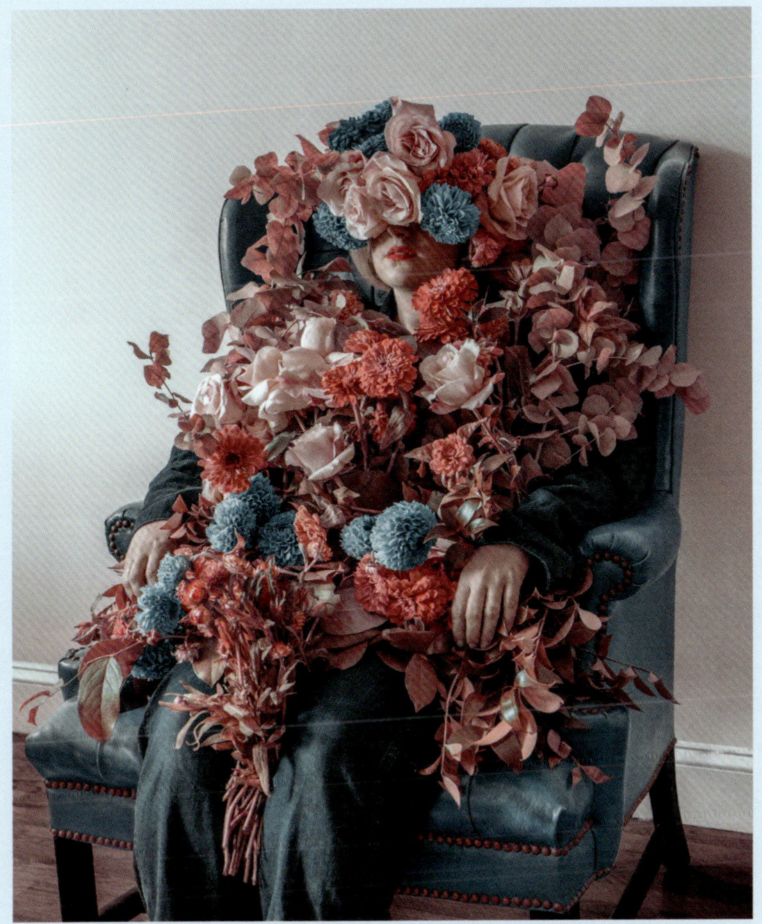

Growing in Odd Directions, Brooke DiDonato, 2018

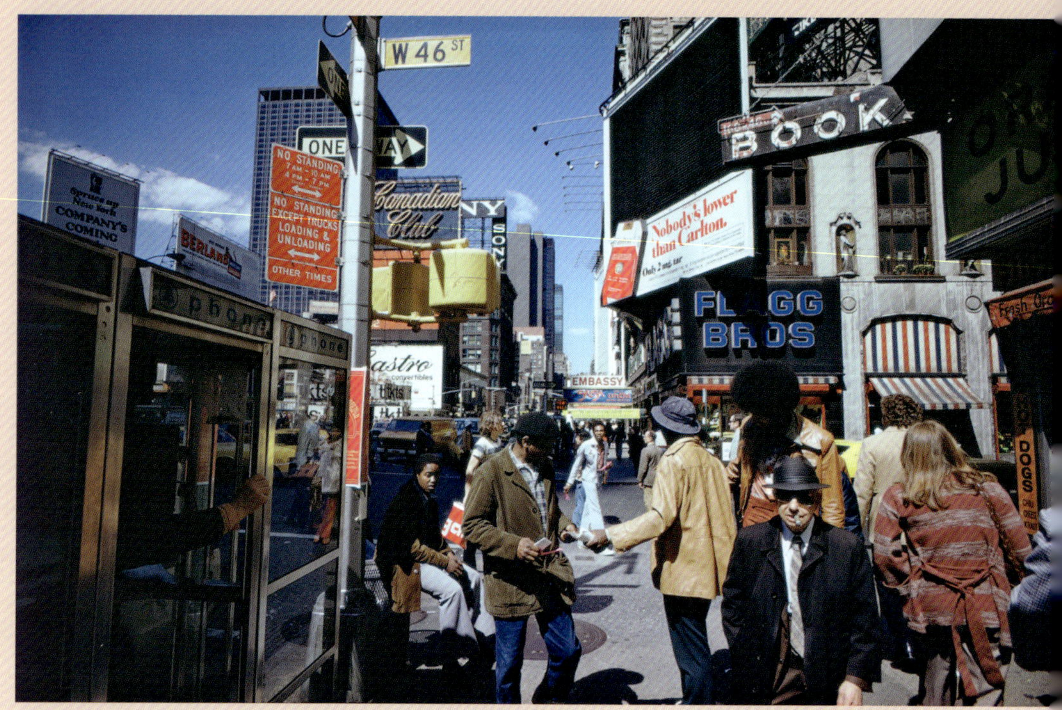

New York City, West 46th Street and Broadway, Joel Meyerowitz, 1976

MULTIPLE NARRATIVES

EXPLORE MANY STORIES AT ONCE

Multiple narratives hold the power to immerse the viewer in a story that is layered, intricate and engaging. The abundance of content in each frame enables multiple stories to be told in a single photograph. Instead of isolating a single subject or moment, a maximalist image can capture numerous events simultaneously, with each one contributing to the bigger picture.[1]

These images overflow with elements to create a sense of depth, complexity and movement; they include several threads that compel the viewer to look more closely at the smaller stories unfolding within. This layered approach resonates as it replicates everyday life, where countless interactions unfold at the same time.[2]

Composition and framing are important aspects to consider when incorporating multiple narratives. With limited space in the frame, every element has the potential to provide information about the unfolding stories. In a maximalist composition, all of these details are at the forefront, competing for attention, so it is essential that they are arranged in a way that is not overly complex or confusing for a viewer; they need to be structured so they enable the audience to understand each narrative.

Joel Meyerowitz's image presents numerous unfolding mini stories on a bustling New York street full of pedestrians, vendors and storefronts. In the foreground, a couple exchanges something, while other figures move past, each absorbed in their own direction and agenda. Behind them, a row of signs and storefronts tower above. Despite the uncertainties, the image has multiple layers of activity, all demanding attention and further investigation.

Timing is crucial when you are working on a multiple narrative composition. It is unlikely to just appear before you, and you will have to start by finding a suitable location that has the potential for several elements to coincide. Then it is a matter of waiting for the right moment, where characters mix or events occur in the same split second. Having the suitable exposure settings pre-set on your camera will ensure you don't miss the moment.

Maximalist photographs that contain multiple narratives will encourage viewers to engage with the image for longer as they discover some of the other sub-plots. Like many of the examples featured in this book, these photographs reward curiosity and repeated viewing, as they reflect the complexity of real-life experiences that often overlap in a shared space.

[1] *See* Multiple Focal Points pp. 20–1

[2] *See* The Everyday pp. 124–5

PORTRAITS

AMPLIFY IDENTITY THROUGH ABUNDANCE

When creating a compelling maximalist portrait, every element should be intentional and deliberate, contributing to the subject's narrative in a meaningful way. Intricate styling and staging – including props, clothing and backgrounds – can help establish a rich visual experience, and each element has the potential to offer an insight into the subject's identity, emotions, background or experiences. A carefully selected object or symbolic setting can introduce layers of meaning that draw the viewer in and deepens their engagement with the image. In maximalist portraiture, these choices are crucial, as every inclusion (or exclusion) shapes the narrative and adds dimension to the subject's identity.[1]

Light, texture, colour and composition play a vital part in shaping how the viewer responds emotionally to an image. Rather than focusing on the subject or isolating them, maximalist portraits often place them within a visually abundant environment that reflects aspects of who they are, while also adding complexity and depth. Composition becomes especially important in navigating this abundance. The relationship between the subject and their surroundings helps to direct the viewer's attention and ensures that the scene remains engaging, rather than overwhelming. When balanced effectively, the composition reveals character and context, not only through the subject, but through everything around them, resulting in a powerful and meaningful portrait.

Horst P Horst's maximalist image offers an alternative approach to a portrait, using repetition, fragmentation and layering to create visual complexity. In this portrait, multiple versions of the same subject appear within a single frame, each with a different expression or pose, but unified through their consistent styling, lighting and elegance. Instead of placing the subject centrally and building detail around them, the photographer chooses to multiply them, allowing the repetition itself to become the source of maximalism. The fragmentation and layering of the image invites an active viewing experience where maximalism becomes a tool to explore subtle differences rather than sheer volume. It is a powerful example of how maximalist portraiture can be refined and conceptual.[2]

[1] *See* Multiple Focal Points pp. 20–1

[2] *See* Repetition pp. 70–1

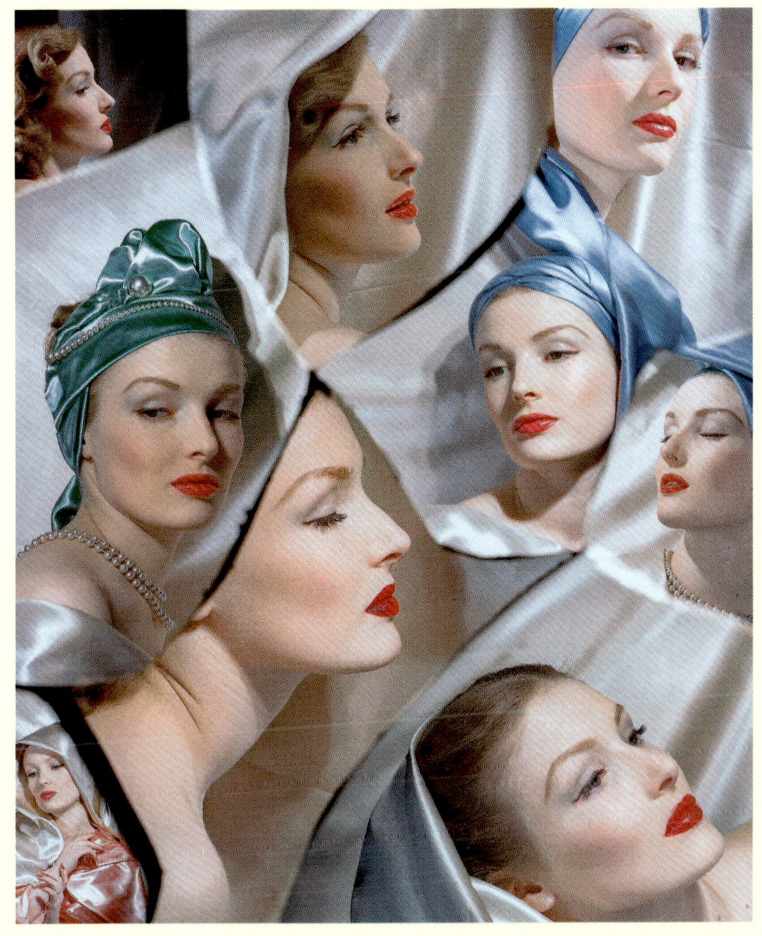

Susann Shaw, Horst P. Horst, 1943

Colour and lighting can significantly enhance the emotional tone and narrative of a maximalist portrait. A thoughtful use of colour – be it complimentary tones or vibrant contrasting palettes – can influence how the audience views the image and connects with the subject. Colour can help set the mood, guide the eye and reinforce the subject's character or emotional state.[3]

Similarly, experimenting with lighting can help shape how a portrait feels. Different lighting approaches can highlight key details or influence the emotional tone: dramatic, directional light can intensify the mood, for example, while softer, diffused lighting can evoke more gentle emotions. These choices can help ensure that the emotion of the portrait remains clear among the abundance of detail.[4]

Anka Zhuravleva's powerful portrait comes vividly to life as the subject's flowing red hair radiates outwards, filling the frame in a way that feels both wild yet intentional. This abundance immediately draws the viewer in, imbuing the portrait with motion, energy and emotion. The vibrant movement of the hair contrasts beautifully with the subject's calm expression and partially obscured face, creating a sense of emotional tension and intrigue. The maximalist approach leverages one single compelling element rather than a cluttered frame to create a captivating and powerful portrait that is full of identity and feeling.

[3] *See* Emotive Colour pp. 48–9

[4] *See* Dynamic Lighting pp. 40–3

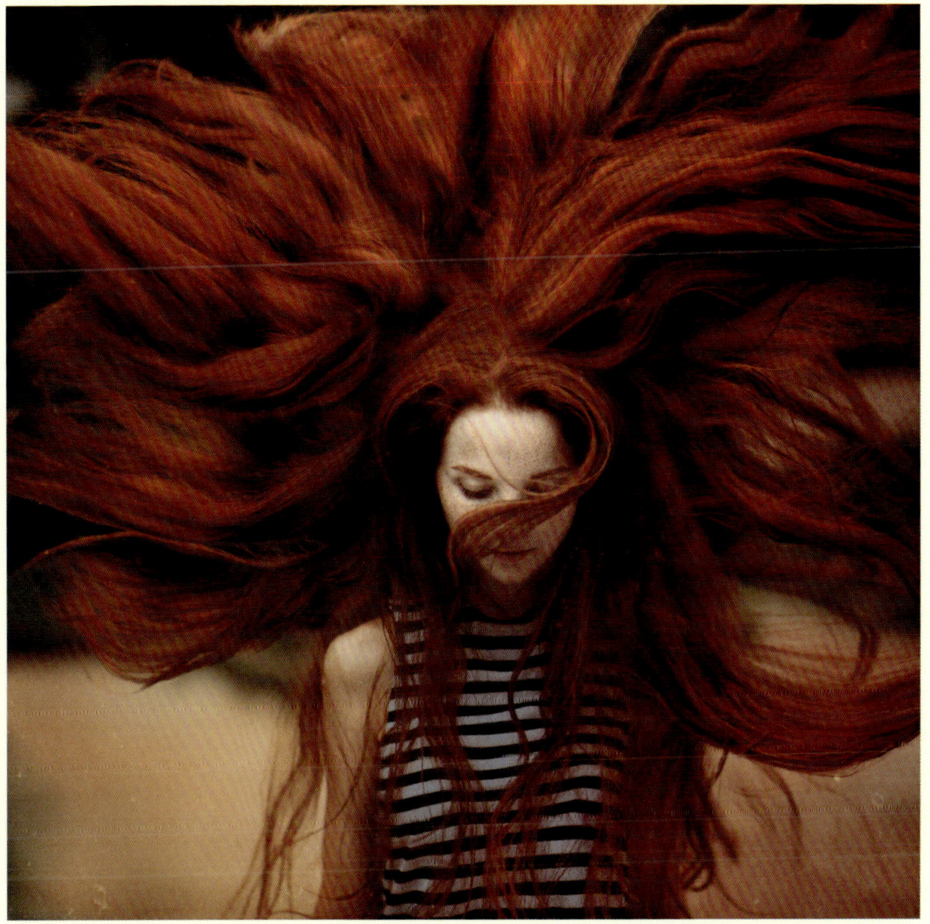

Sunny Katia, Anka Zhuravleva, 2014

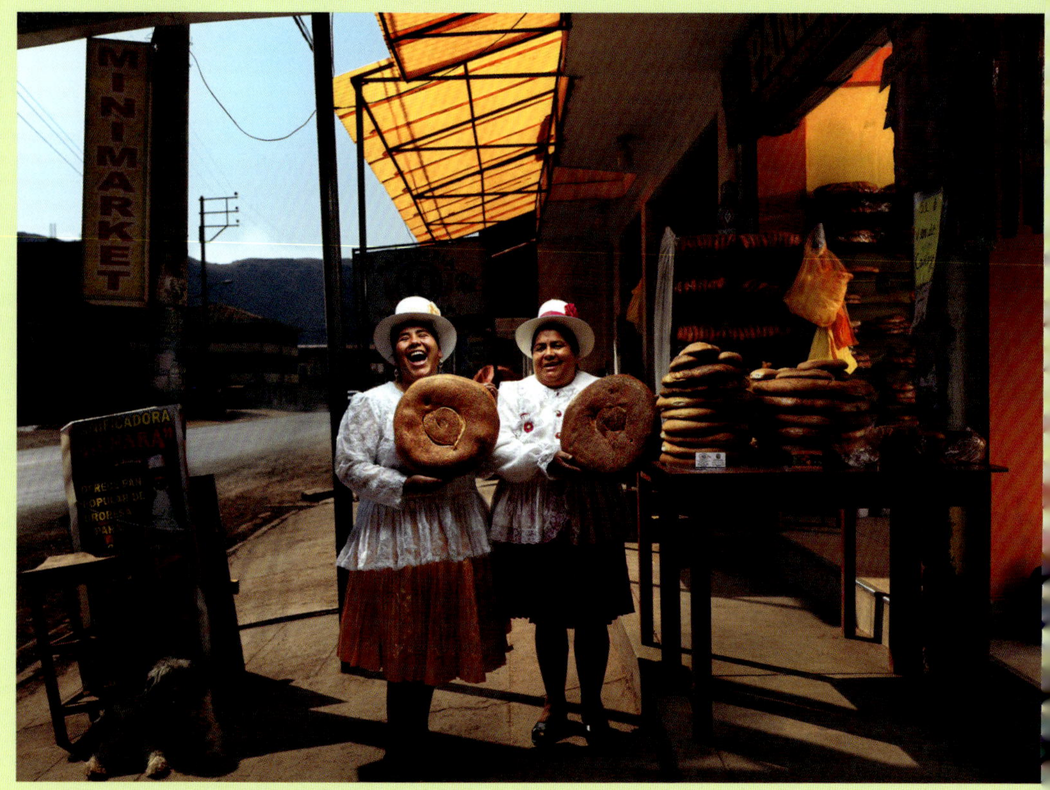

Nilda Luz Licona Ojeda and Fortunata Licon, Bakers Oropesa, Peru, Roman Jehanno, 2019

TELL A STORY THROUGH THE RICHNESS OF DETAIL

Through carefully composed layers of objects, textures and symbols, an image can tell stories that reach beyond the surface of the frame. Rather than isolating a single moment or subject, maximalism offers space for multiple elements of a ceremony, custom or everyday cultural practice to coexist within the frame. This immersive visual language creates a sensory experience that conveys not just the appearance, but also the atmosphere, emotions and meaning embedded in tradition.

A key strength to this approach lies in its ability to draw the viewer in, encouraging them to look beyond the surface of the image. Layering visual elements can help tell a complex story, and a single frame might include people, gestures, objects, patterns and interactions that work together to build a broader, more intricate portrait of a cultural or ceremonial event.

In Roman Jehanno's image, the subjects – two daughters of a baker – joyfully present large local breads, dressed in traditional Peruvian clothing that reflects their cultural heritage. They stand in front of their family's bakery, which is overflowing with colour and goods. The scene bursts with life, feeling and detail, from the stacked breads to the warm saturated tones that fill the frame. Every object contributes to the story of an everyday moment of celebration, tradition and community. This image creates a powerful impression that invites the viewer not just to observe, but to immerse themself in a shared cultural routine that is both festive and deeply rooted in place and identity.[1]

A single maximalist image can capture more than just people. Including more of the surrounding details in an image provides the audience with a broad overview of a particular culture, with each element telling us something about the values, history and way of life of the subjects. It is the photographer's task to capture these details and allow them to contribute to the narrative of that tradition.

Authenticity plays a vital role in this process. While an image could be staged or styled, the most resonant photographs are often true-to-life and of real cultural significance. This means that while the composition cannot be easily controlled or arranged, its authenticity results in an image that conveys a genuine sense of lived experience. It is these photographs that provide the viewer with a genuine invitation to engage with a culture and its complex traditions, that capture their richness and encourage a deeper appreciation of their spirit and meaning.[2]

[1] *See* Symbolism pp. 118–19

[2] *See* Layered Meanings pp. 134–5

SYMBOLISM

LAYER MEANING THROUGH VISUAL CLUES

In Rena Effendi's photograph, a tabletop overflows with vibrant pink rose petals, while a group of hands delicately sort through the flowers. Taken during Morocco's annual rose harvest, the image captures a deeply rooted cultural ritual. Every spring, women gather to hand-sort petals for distillation into rose oil or water, or to dry for garlands.[1] Although documentary in nature, the image is rich in symbolic meaning and sensory significance. Roses are associated with love and beauty, and their abundance multiplies their effect. The repetition of hands, each slightly different in gesture and skin tone, implies unity in diversity. There is no single focal point, but the layered content invites the viewer to explore and interpret.

This is the power of symbolism in photography, where a meaning can be suggested through density and layering. A frame that contains a visual abundance of information and details can reveal complex meanings in many ways: through multiple objects, gestures, colours, textures, light or other visual clues, and the relationships between those elements. Such symbolism is cumulative, so meaning is built up and conveyed through repetition, juxtaposition and saturation, and multiple symbols can be combined to form associations rather than a singular message. These can be metaphorical, or have more direct, obvious links to the story or explanation.

Creating symbolically rich images begins with intent: deciding what to include or omit. What is the concept or emotion that you want to express in the image? Once this is identified, the composition should layer the visual elements that help convey this meaning. Colour, texture, props, lighting and positioning can reinforce this core message, while repetition and intentional excess have the potential to instill multiple meanings without them becoming confusing or chaotic. Incorporating symbols that can be interpreted both literally and metaphorically will generally be more immersive for the viewer, as reflection and curiosity may lead to a particular emotion.

[1] *See* Tradition pp. 116–17

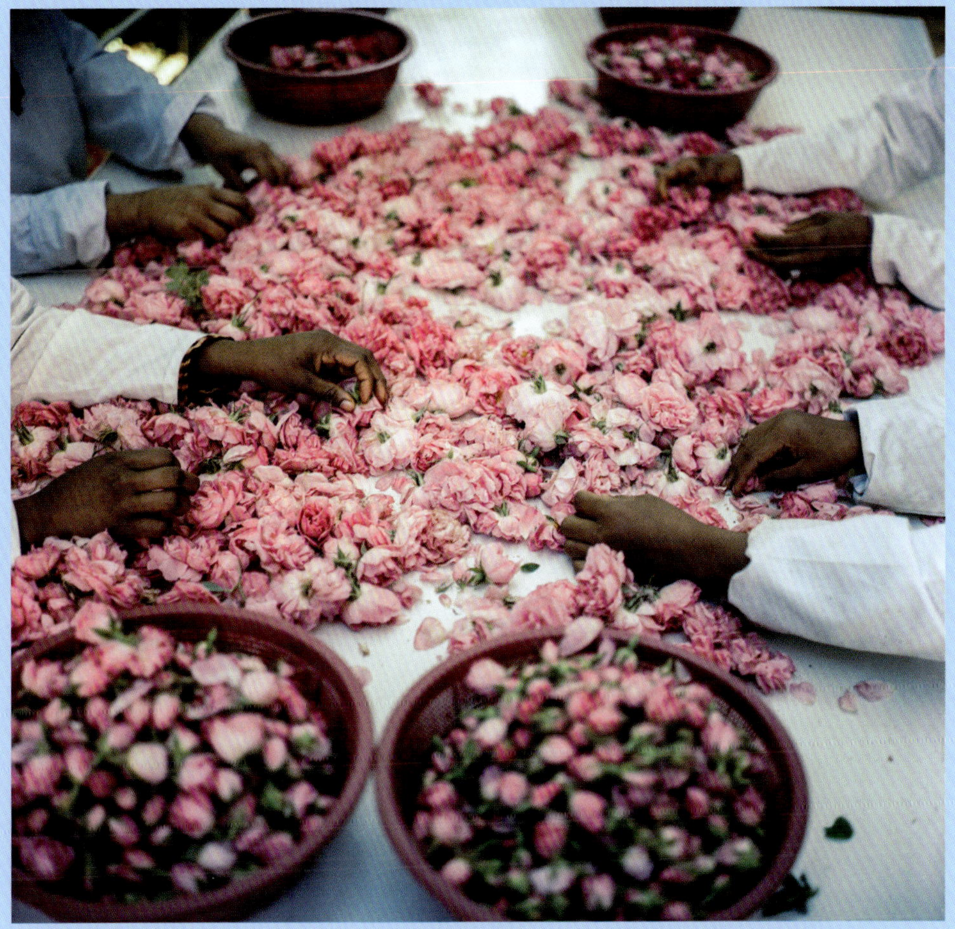

Petal Pushers, Kalaat M'Gouna, Morocco, Rena Effendi, 2024

SYMBOLISM

In Brooke Shaden's *Moth to a Flame*, the image leans heavily into figurative symbolism. Multiples of the same person are seemingly drawn towards a glowing flame in the middle of a burning forest, captured in an emotive, cinematic style. The act of moving towards the light is symbolic of the human impulse to pursue something, or a passion that may ultimately consume us. Here, the interplay of darkness and illumination, and the immersive atmosphere, creates a layered visual narrative. The abundance in this image is not found in clutter, but in the emotional density and weight of layered meaning, dramatic tone and evocative form. Each element contributes to the symbolic visual language that translates into a poetic, haunting image.[2]

Symbolic meaning becomes effective when the frame is filled with objects, people, gestures and details that convey ideas and invite deeper exploration. Each element, despite perhaps seeming merely decorative, can hold a deeper significance. Even the colour palette can symbolize a mood or cultural reference, adding an extra layer of emotion.[3] In maximalist photography, it is the abundance of these elements that allows a more complex and varied approach to symbolism. This encourages the viewer to engage with the image from multiple perspectives and to interpret the meaning that has been carefully included in the frame.

Compositionally, the elements should still be positioned thoughtfully throughout the frame. The way they interact will inevitably contribute to a sense of balance, tension or perhaps even contradiction. Including extra details may result in more complexity, but it is essential that some framework or structure is put in place to help convey this elaborate narrative. Placing symbolic objects, colours and figures so they interact with one another will not only amplify the overall theme, but also make the image easier to understand and interpret. It is not about one object or a single symbol sitting in isolation, but about how everything within the frame works to create a deeper, more profound meaning.

[2] *See* Multiple Focal Points pp. 20–1
[3] *See* Layered Meanings pp. 134–5

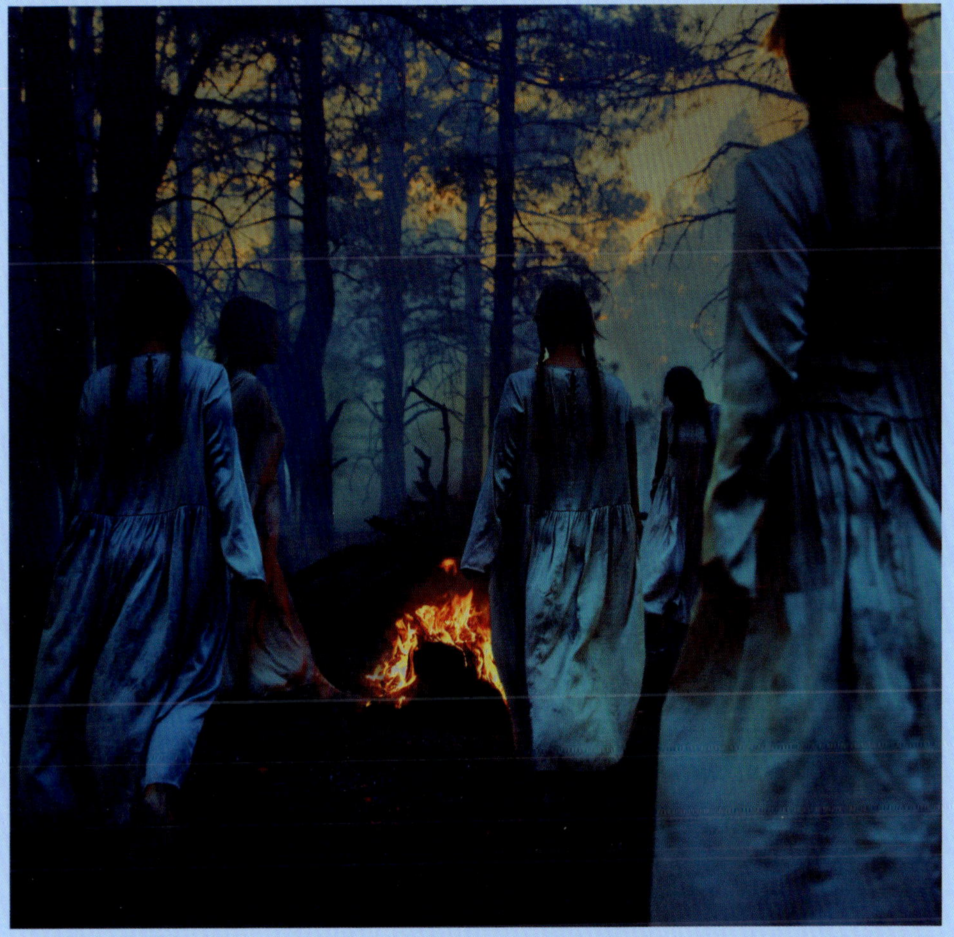

Moth to a Flame, Brooke Shaden, 2024

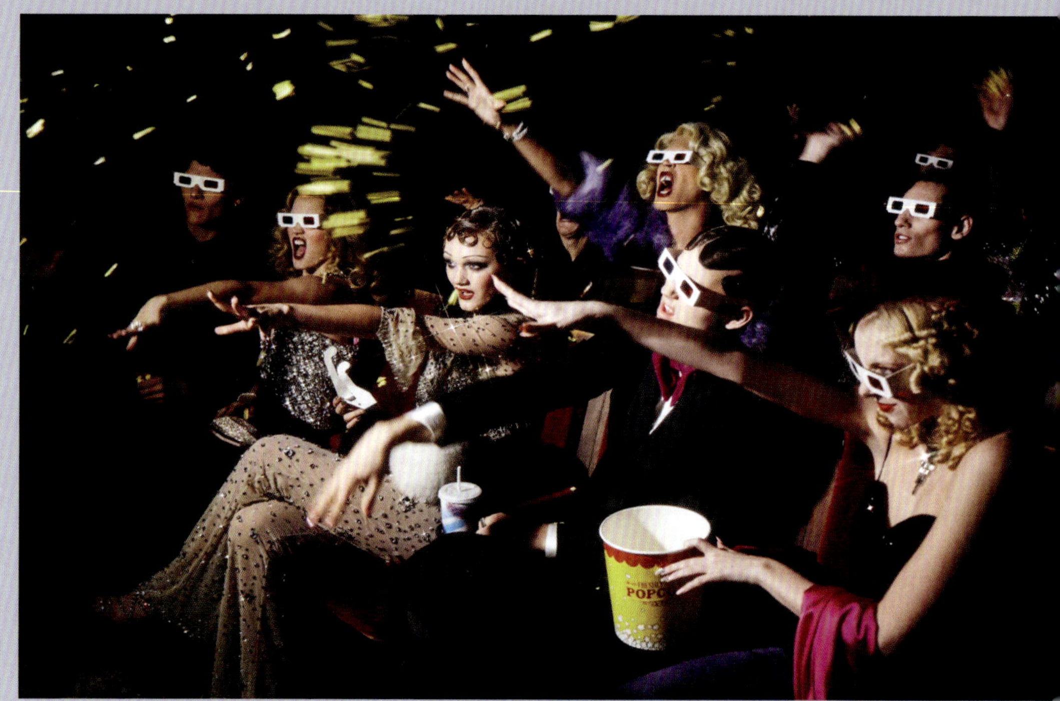

Booh!, New York (Metrograph Cinema), Ellen Von Unwerth, 2018

THEATRICAL

FIND DRAMA IN EVERY DETAIL

In Ellen Von Unwerth's striking image, a group of people are captured sitting together in a dark cinema. The subjects appear larger than life, with dramatic expressions, exaggerated gestures and elegant evening gowns; every detail aligns with the idea of a performance in progress, full of energy and emotion. The result is a fun and captivating image and it feels as though we are witnessing a grand scene unfolding, complete with an enthusiastic audience and spilled popcorn.[1] The theatrical quality of the image is enhanced by the interaction between the elements within the frame, with the subjects, fabrics, colour and setting coming together to create an experience that feels intense, emotionally charged and cinematic.

The theatrical mood is heightened by the lighting, which does more than simply illuminate the scene. Instead of flat or even lighting, the photographer has chosen to use dramatic, directional lighting that isolates certain characters and casts deep shadows, like a spotlight on a stage. In the context of maximalist abundance, this lighting is effective in creating mood and building atmosphere, but also in guiding the viewer's attention around the scene.

Theatrical compositions evoke a sense of drama, exaggeration and emotion through their intricate designs and setups. They draw inspiration from the grand nature of theatre, combining the elements of staging and lighting to create an image that feels as if it exists within a larger ongoing story. Instead of simply documenting a scene, you create an image that feels as if it's unfolding on a stage, where each element contributes to the idea of a show.

At the heart of this approach is the idea of creating a world within the frame – one that seems to unfold beyond the edges of the image, just as a theatrical performance might expand beyond the stage.[2] Every object becomes part of the story, and props, costumes and set design become central to establishing the visual narrative and emotional context of the image.

Another hallmark of theatrical compositions is the heightened emotion they convey. Subjects often appear mid-gesture, and these gestures act as focal points that guide the viewer through the scene, exploring the costumes, props and other elements. The sense of performance also encourages a deeper engagement with the viewer, asking them to think about the unfolding story and to imagine what came before and what might happen next.

[1] *See* Playfulness pp. 106–9
[2] *See* Breaking the Edges pp. 72–3

THE EVERYDAY

LAYER THE BEAUTY OF DAILY LIFE

Some of the most compelling images are found in the unassuming areas of daily life. When approached with attention and openness, everyday environments become rich, layered portraits of human existence. This is where maximalism becomes less about design and staging and takes on a more documentary approach, with every object and element adding a layer of information that contributes to the visual overload and narratives of daily life.

This spirit is captured perfectly in Ryosuke Kosuge's image of a tightly packed shop in Tokyo's Akihabara District. It is overflowing with boxes, gadgets and objects stacked close together, crowding the frame and creating a sense of density and tunnel vision that draws the eye inwards. At the centre, a man is smiling warmly, leaning on the counter as if inviting the viewer into his world. Like a customer stepping into the scene, the viewer is immersed in the texture, noise and familiarity. The human connection is key: the man's gaze bridges the gap between the scene and the viewer, and anchors the chaos. This isn't just an image of a shop, it's a layered portrait of the man's life, where passion, work and identity surround him in the small space.[1]

Approaching images of daily life will inevitably involve complexity and detail, and will naturally immerse an audience. By finding frames that feel dense and lived-in, the images gain character and reveal their inner stories. The narrative feels stronger because there are countless small details, each hinting at its own piece of the bigger picture. The more details that are included, the more questions are raised; each object becomes a clue, inviting the viewer to explore further. By filling the frame with abundance, the photographer encourages the viewer to appreciate the richness of the world around them and to see beauty in the ordinary things that are often overlooked.

Photographing the everyday in this way requires a thoughtful composition, but it is not about artificially tidying or simplifying a scene. The key is not to clear the space but to embrace its complexity. Balance is essential, and you will need to ensure that the maximalist frame is not too chaotic or confusing. Layers and framing are important, and a clear point of focus among a detailed foreground or background can help tell the story. Wide-angle lenses will help you capture more of the environment, which can immerse the viewer more deeply in the scene.[2] A small aperture ensures all of the elements in the scene remain in sharp focus, reinforcing the clarity of the complex composition.

[1] *See* Portraits pp. 112–15
[2] *See* Framing pp. 66–7

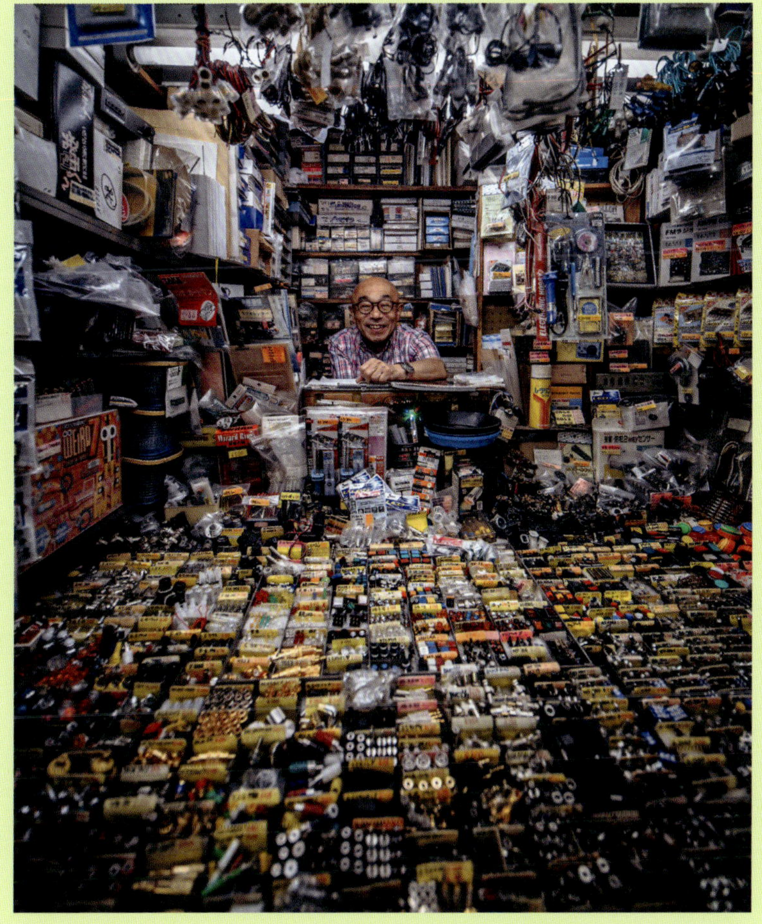

Japanese Narrow Dense Store, RK, 2017

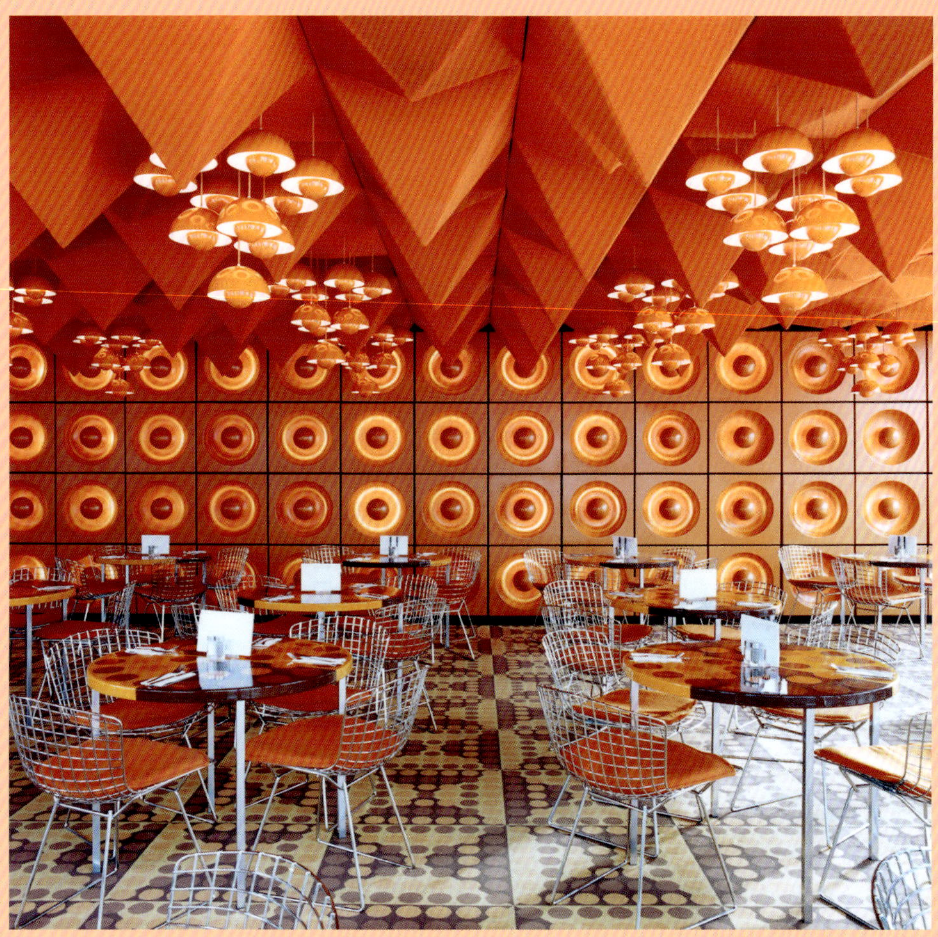

Spiegelkantine Hamburg IV 2000, Candida Höfer, 2000

CAPTURE HOW A SPACE FEELS

In Candida Höfer's image of the cafeteria at the Spiegel publishing house, we see a striking example of how maximalist principles can be applied with precision. Every surface is covered in bold, contrasting patterns and textures that are connected through their vibrant orange hues, creating a dynamic tension between order and chaos. Repeating lines, textures and motifs form a structure within the visual complexity, resulting in a dynamic tension in the photograph.

Rather than isolating or simplifying elements, the photographer embraces the complexity within the space, capturing it in a way that feels immersive, organized and atmospheric. The result is a scene that balances intensity with emotional warmth. There is visual impact and sensory overload, but also a clear intention behind the design.

Photographing interior spaces offers a rich opportunity to explore visual abundance. The structure and decor of these spaces provides a framework, but the contents reveal the character of the occupants or users and hint at their daily life, habits and routines.

When photographing maximalist interiors, take time to immerse yourself in the environment. Observe how the different elements relate to one another and look for points of visual rhythm. In particular, repeating elements can serve as visual anchors and give the scene structure, helping to create a sense of order within the abundance.[1]

Carefully consider your viewpoint, perspective and framing. Wide-angle shots can showcase the full expanse of a room and emphasize the density of information, but this can risk flattening the image. Sometimes, a tighter frame will allow you to close in on a particularly dense area, which can be more impactful.[2]

Lighting is another key factor. Natural light is ideal for interiors, creating shadows and highlights that reveal depth. However, combining natural and artificial light can work well when trying to illuminate darker corners of a space.

Importantly, resist the urge to over-style or tidy the space, as smaller details contribute to the sense of authenticity that makes this type of photography compelling. It is not necessarily about perfection, but about presence: how the space is used and not just how it looks.

[1] *See* Repetition pp. 70–1
[2] *See* Framing pp. 66–7

FOOD

PHOTOGRAPH THE PROCESS, NOT JUST THE PLATE

Kitchens and food preparation spaces provide a rich and layered subject for maximalist exploration. These are spaces inherently full of life, where everyday function and routine combine with expression, colour, texture and movement to create a vibrant and often chaotic harmony.

Cooking is one of the most expressive and sensory aspects of home life, and visually it can result in wonderfully emotive images. While food photography is often associated with precision and styling, maximalist food imagery embraces the wider scene – the mess, spills and movements that give context to its preparation. Kitchens, pantries and worktops are ideal hunting grounds for an abundance of visual material, be it worn utensils, half-prepped produce or textured surfaces.

In this compelling photograph, a kitchen countertop becomes the main focal point. However, it documents more than just a kitchen scene – it captures the act of creation in progress. The sprawling countertop is covered with a spread of scattered ingredients, half-used bowls and utensils, evoking a sense of warmth and creation. It is not just about what is being made but the experience of making it. There is a sense of joy, messiness and human presence that makes the photograph immersive and relatable. The resulting image is both beautiful and expressive, capturing an emotionally charged scene for the viewer.[1]

When photographing food scenes in this way, it is important to resist the urge to overly control or style the scene. Embrace the authenticity of the process and try to allow the space to evolve naturally. The mess, movement and disorder are all part of the narrative, and these imperfections will result in strong visual stories that are more relatable for the audience than those staged for the camera.

Think about layering the image through depth and composition. Cooking will inevitably result in a natural buildup of layers, such as utensils and ingredients, and these can be framed in an intentional way to create structure. Position your subject at the centre of the scene and focus with intent, either using a shallow depth of field to draw focus to a specific area of interest or a small aperture to keep more of the scene sharp.

Texture and light will help define how a kitchen scene or meal feels to the viewer. Natural light is often ideal, as it reveals surface qualities gently and casts soft shadows. Food photography is ultimately not just about visual appeal, but about the act of making and the context that surrounds it.

[1] *See* Multiple Focal Points pp. 20–1

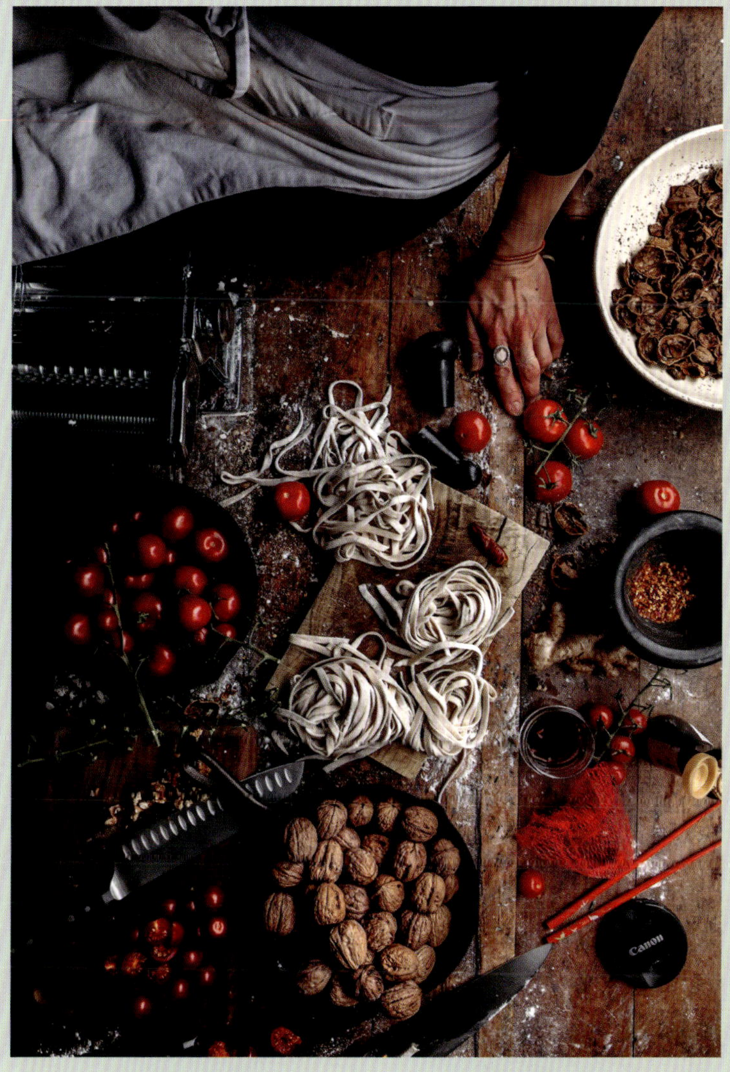

Red, Betty Shin Binon, 2023

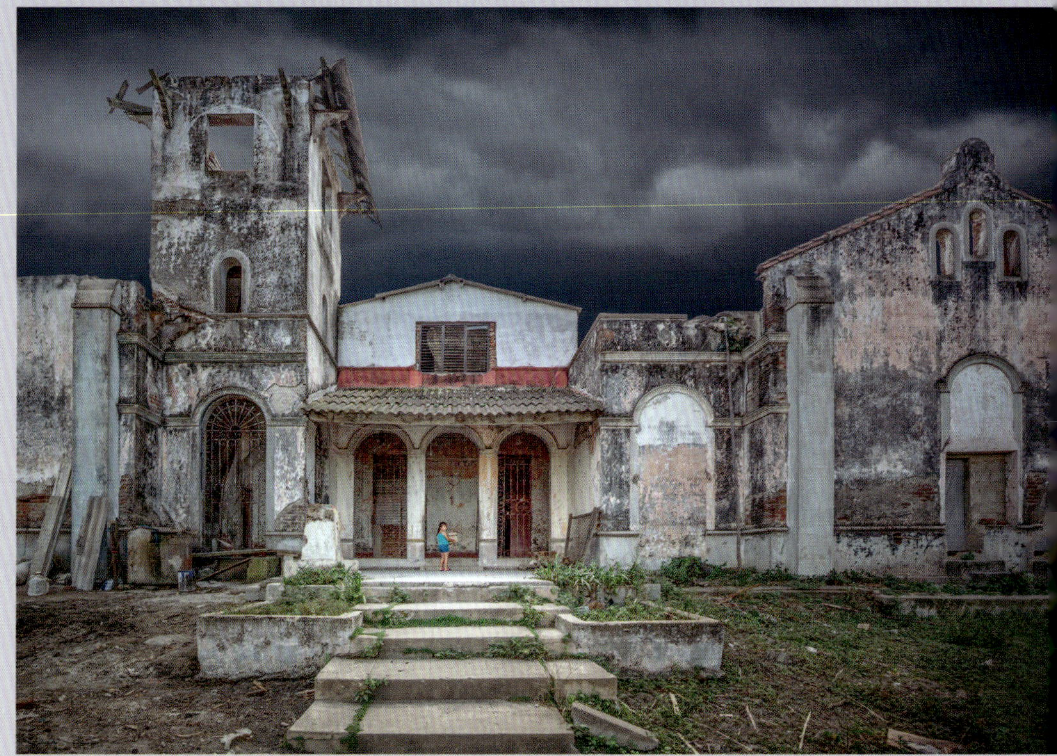

Looking Back, Antony Zacharias, 2017

JUXTAPOSITION

CREATE CONTRASTS FOR VISUAL IMPACT

In this image, a crumbling building dominates the foreground under a dark, stormy sky. The weathered facade and broken towers hint at its former glory, now faded through time and neglect. Peeling paint and missing roof sections reveal a state of ruin, yet at the centre, a young girl stands quietly near the entrance, looking directly at the camera. Her small figure contrasts sharply with the massive, decaying structure behind her. This contrast between human vulnerability and architectural ruins gives the image emotional weight. Rather than simply showing an abandoned place, the presence of the girl adds a deeper layer that highlights both the desolation of the building and the quiet strength of those still living in such harsh conditions.[1]

Juxtaposition involves placing contrasting elements side by side to heighten their impact. These contrasts can appear in many forms – colour, scale, texture, mood, age and subject matter – but it is the deliberate combination of these differences that gives the image its energy and depth. By layering these oppositions in a single frame, the image sparks curiosity and tension, prompting the viewer to pause and interpret what they see. It's not merely about contrast for its own sake, but about using differences to tell a deeper, more layered story.

There are several techniques that can be used to help reinforce the power of juxtaposition in a maximalist image. With so many competing details, it's important to ensure that both the message and the viewer's focus do not get lost within the visual abundance. Subtle visual clues, such as differences in scale, material, texture or colour, can help guide the viewer's eye gently towards the contrasting elements.

The emotional impact of juxtaposition cannot be overstated. By positioning elements with strong emotional suggestions next to one another, you can create feelings that stay with the viewer long after they have looked away. These images go beyond visual interest and invite the audience to reflect, question or feel something deeper.[2]

The way in which juxtaposition functions in maximalist photography also reflects a more metaphorical sense of abundance. It's not just about filling the frame, it's about capturing the layered, often contradictory nature of the world around us. By bringing together contrasting elements, an image can reflect the complexities of human experience and the richness found in everyday life.

Ultimately, juxtaposition is a powerful tool for visual storytelling. The contrasts in the frame can create narrative possibilities that invite the viewer to ask questions and imagine connections.

[1] *See* Multiple Focal Points pp. 20–1
[2] *See* Layered Meanings pp. 134–5

AMBIGUITY

LEAVE ROOM FOR INTERPRETATION

Images that are rich in detail thrive on ambiguity – the idea that not every detail has to be explained or resolved. An abundant frame that is packed with objects, textures and visual cues can hint at multiple stories or contexts without ever revealing enough information for a clear or defined narrative.[1] This approach works well in visually complex scenes as it is natural for a viewer to want to make sense of what they see, even when faced with a cluttered or layered composition. By filling the frame with a mixture of seemingly random elements, or withholding context or other environmental clues, you can create images that invite curiosity, speculation and personal interpretation, each of which draws the viewer in more deeply.

Subtle compositional anchors can help you maintain a sense of ambiguity without the image becoming too random, chaotic or disassociated. These anchors could be a central element or main focal point, or a particular colour palette, random pattern or consistent lighting that helps to unite the scene. In either case, they will prevent the viewer from getting entirely lost in the disarray, even if you are not revealing any clues about the story or narrative. It is this uncertainty that ensures the image remains engaging, rather than frustrating.

Lockdown, by Marta Bevacqua, appears to capture a garden space filled with furniture, appliances and other random items that have no obvious connection. Each object – be it the open book, kettle or crash helmet – encourages the viewer to draw their own conclusions, but there is no definitive answer in the frame. It is this ambiguity that makes the image so compelling: elements that don't obviously relate to one another raise questions, prompting the viewer to try and interpret what they are looking at.[2]

The ambiguity of this partial information hints at a broader context without fully revealing it. In a maximalist composition, there are many such clues, each offering a different path towards a possible explanation. The elements in your images don't have to be clear and sharp, though. If they are captured slightly blurred through fleeting motion, or partially obscured or in shadow, you will still create a similar ambiguity and uncertain connection for your audience. The result is an image that feels alive with potential stories: a puzzle where the pieces don't quite fit into a single picture.

[1] *See* Multiple Narratives pp. 110–11

[2] *See* Symbolism pp. 118–21

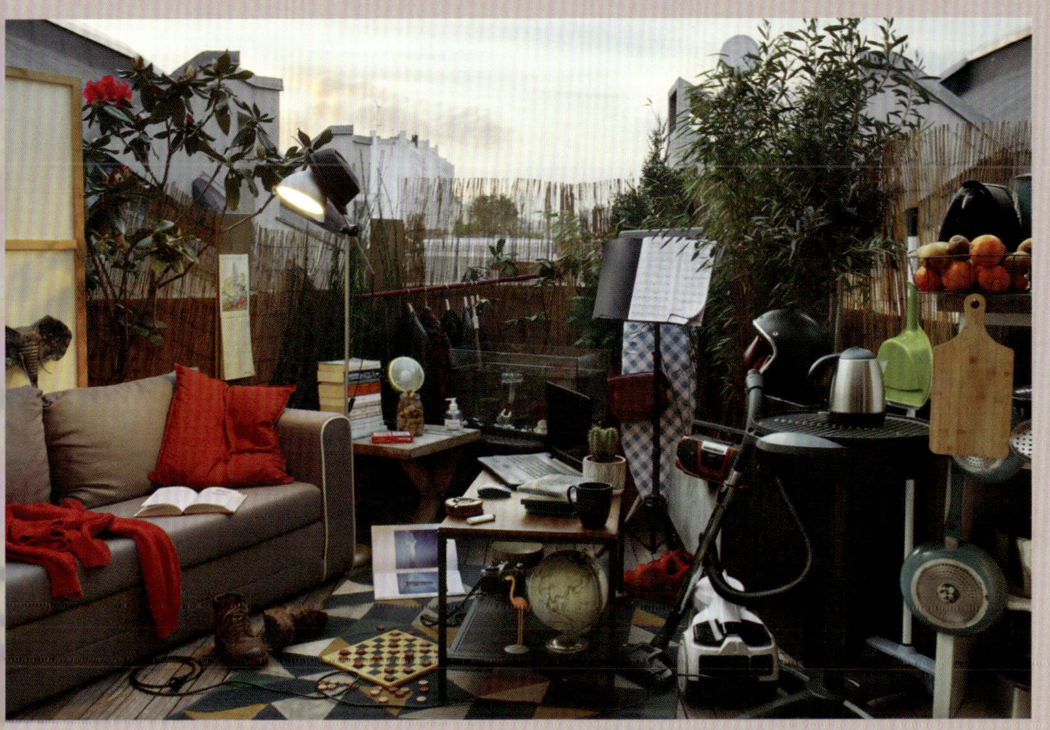

'Lockdown' Alternative Solution: In Need of Air, Paris, Marta Bevacqua, 2020

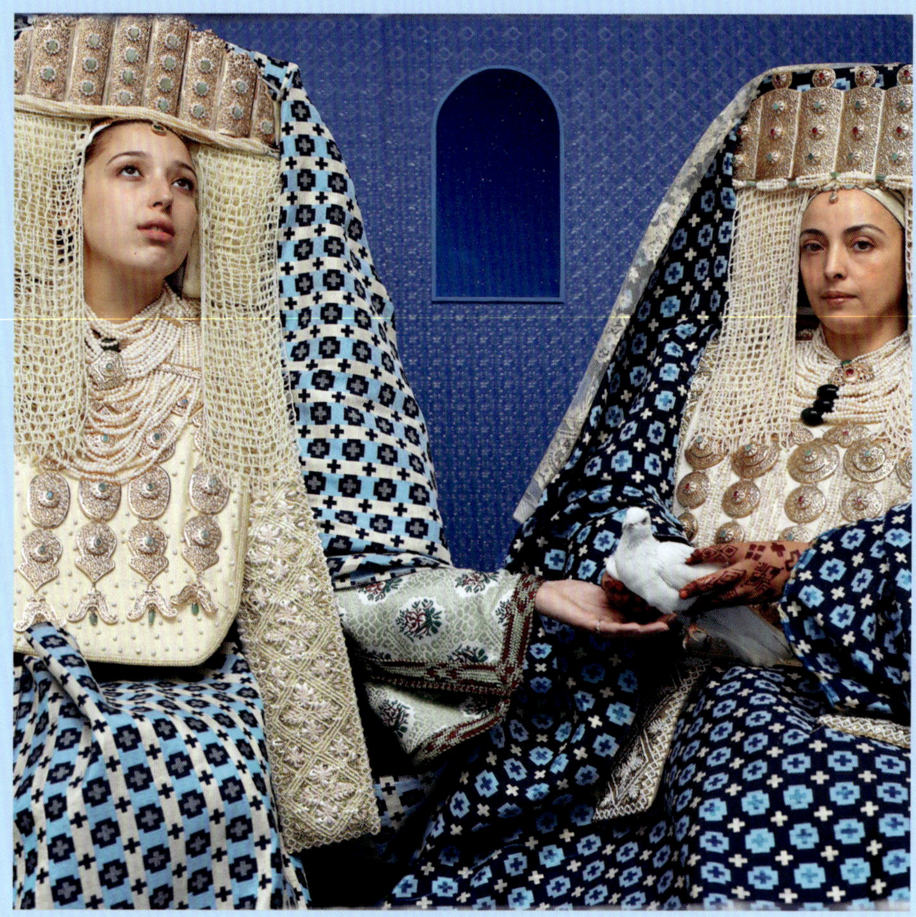

Marhouna, from the Dry Land series, Sara Aït Benabdallah, 2025

LAYERED MEANINGS

BUILD A STORY THROUGH CONNECTION

In *Marhouna*, Sara Aït Benabdallah captures a powerful and visually dense portrait that blends maximalist aesthetics through symbolism, repetition and richly layered visual cues. Two Moroccan women occupy the frame, dressed in ornate, almost regal clothing beside a similarly patterned backdrop. Their presence is commanding and their expressions are composed; they are solemn, yet thoughtful. One has hennaed hands and is holding a white dove – a universal symbol of peace. The scene feels historical or ceremonial, but on closer inspection, it reveals a deliberate staging that blurs the line between the real and the constructed. The maximalist approach intensifies the sense of meaning within each layer, object or item, and encourages the viewer to question the roles these elements play. There is not a single definitive or obvious message, but suggested connections between feminine strength, culture, history, tradition and identity.[1]

Layered meanings emerge when multiple elements in a scene appear to convey different, yet interconnected ideas or stories; where the subject, background or other objects suggest a certain idea or narrative that remains open to interpretation.[2] This is achieved by balancing the density of elements with a clear and coherent arrangement: too many items may lead to confusion and a weaker story or message, while too few can feel uncertain or undeveloped. Consider the narratives of the elements and how they combine to tell the overall story, and think about their position in the frame – grouping them or using colours can help guide the viewer to explore the image in a logical way.[3]

In a portrait, layered meanings can also be seen in how the subject interacts with their environment. Here, body language, posture and gaze all communicate strong implied meaning. In a maximalist setting – where the frame is full of detail – these interactions will gain greater importance and become powerful guides that encourage the viewer to interpret the narrative in the surrounding complexity.[4]

Colour and texture play an important role in hinting at layered meanings. Vibrant tones or subdued colours will affect the mood and emotion of the image, while textural contrasts can contribute in a metaphorical way – rough textures can allude to tension and discomfort, for example.

Lighting can be used to emphasize certain aspects of a scene – those that are important can appear brighter, while those of lesser importance can be left to fade into the shadows. Strategic shadows can also create a sense of depth or mystery, and imply there is more information lurking in the darkness.[5]

[1] *See* Symbolism pp. 118–21
[2] *See* Multiple Narratives pp. 110–11
[3] *See* Multiple Focal Points pp. 20–1
[4] *See* Portraits pp. 112–15
[5] *See* Dynamic Lighting pp. 40–43

ENERGY IN STILLNESS

BALANCE CHAOS WITH MOMENTS OF CALM

'Energy in stillness' might sound contradictory at first, especially in the context of maximalism. However, it is this tension that makes these photographs so compelling. When an image is full of detail, colour and texture, yet also possesses a sense of calm, an audience will stop and linger as they try to decipher what is going on and why.

This stillness will not negate the energy of the scene, but merely provides a focal point that seems to resonate with the surrounding complexities of the environment. Harry Gruyaert masters this effect in the image opposite, which captures a busy Indian urban environment. The frame is filled with an array of people and vehicles going about their everyday life and there is a multitude of overlapping narratives among this abundance. Within the scene, certain figures seem momentarily paused: a man leans on a railing gazing outwards, while others appear frozen in their everyday tasks or interactions. The scene seems packed with activity and yet it is these quieter gestures that anchor the composition. Their stillness doesn't diminish the surrounding energy, but actually seems to enhance it.

At its core, energy in stillness relies on a subtle balance between the dynamic elements of a photograph and the stillness that visually anchors them.[1] Where there is something that should be moving that appears momentarily paused, the entire image can take on a mediative quality. The viewer senses both the flow of life and the solitary instant that seems to pause it, which creates a tension and contrast that is both exhilarating and calming.

The challenge is to compose the frame so that the eye naturally gravitates to that calm centre within the visual abundance. In a maximalist frame full of objects and movement, this can prove tricky, as the calm area can be easily overlooked. Leading lines, contrasting lighting or even colour can help guide the viewer towards this focal point, ensuring it doesn't get lost in the crowd,[2] while post-production techniques such as selective dodging, vignetting or subtle saturation adjustments can also highlight key areas.

Timing is crucial. When you might spot a potential composition in a busy location you will often have to wait for the precise moment when someone pauses, or an otherwise bustling area experiences a brief lull. This doesn't mean the whole scene should appear static. In fact, it works best when the background movement continues, as capturing a moment of stillness within an otherwise active scene highlights the existence of fleeting moments of calm among ceaseless energy.[3]

[1] *See* Quiet Moments pp. 90–3
[2] *See* Leading Lines pp. 18–19
[3] *See* Beauty in Chaos pp. 86–9

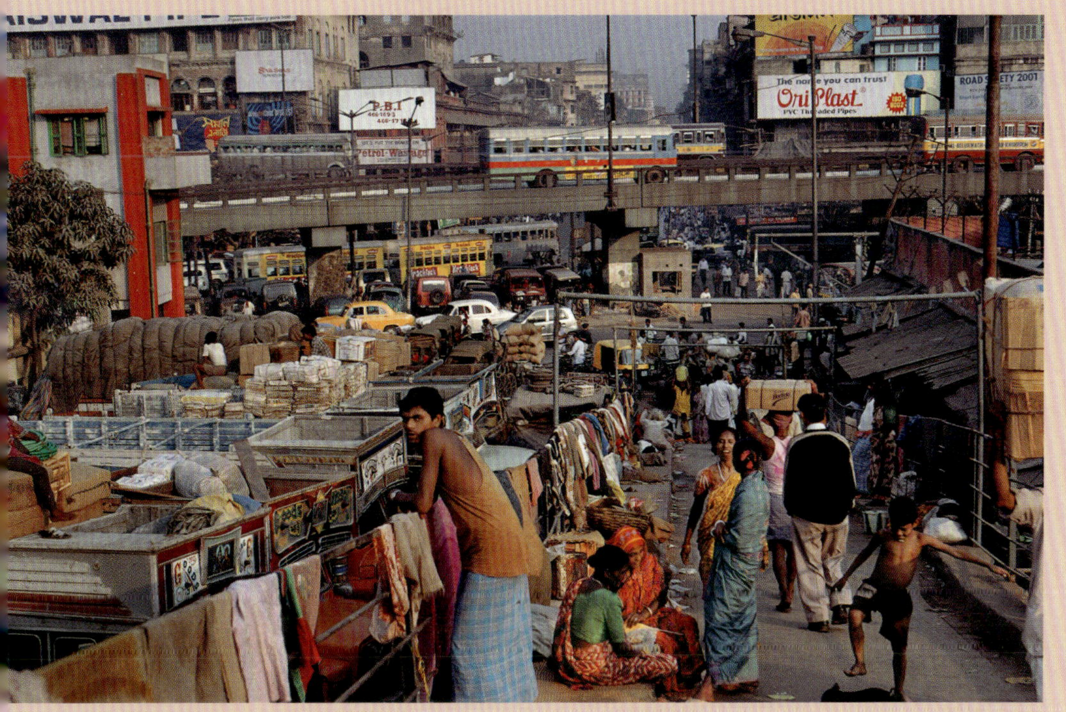

India, Maharashtra, Pune, Harry Gruyaert, 1986

Unless otherwise credited, all photographs are the author's own.

12 Andreas Gursky/VG Bild-Kunst, Bonn. Courtesy Sprüth Magers
16 © Jeffrey Milstein
20 © Alex Webb/Magnum Photos
41 Sarah van Rij
46 Atong Atem, *Blue Face*, 2021, digital photograph, 120 x 159cm, edition of 10 + 2 AP. Courtesy of MARS Gallery and the artist
50 © Patty Carroll www.pattycarroll.com
54 Thandiwe Muriu/Institute
58 Lindsay Adler Photography
63 Album/Alamy Stock Photo
65 © 2025 ARS, NY and DACS, London
74 *Ahmed Legs*, framed photography by © Hassan Hajjaj, 2022/1443 Part of the *Legs* series. Courtesy of Hassan Hajjaj Studio & 193 Gallery, Paris/France
77 Courtesy the artist and JP Morgan Chase Bank
89 Eve Dorfice of Echo Fine Arts
90 Janet Delaney
95 Eurêka, Cath Simard, 2020
97 Pauline Ballet/FFT
101 Christy Lee Rogers www.christyleerogers.com
102 © ALEX PRAGER, Courtesy Alex Prager Studio and Lehmann Maupin, New York, Seoul and London
104 Jovana Rikalo
107 © Maisie Cousins. All rights reserved 2025/Bridgeman Images

PICTURE CREDITS

109 Brooke DiDonato
110 © Joel Meyerowitz, Courtesy Howard Greenberg Gallery
113 Horst P. Horst, Vogue © Condé Nast
115 Anka Zhuravleva, "Sunny Katya"/Ekaterina, 2011
116 Roman Jehanno, romanjehanno.com
119 © Rena Effendi
121 Brooke Shaden (www.brookeshaden.com)
122 Ellen von Unwerth/Trunk Archive
125 Photo by RK (Instagram: @rkrkrk)
126 © Candida Höfer/VG Bild-Kunst, Bonn 2025
129 Betty Shin Binon, Stems and Forks. This photograph was captured for a short video shot by Betty Shin Binon, inspired by Krysztof Kiéslowski's *Three Colours* trilogy, specifically *Three Colours: Red (1994)*. It symbolizes the chaos of mistakes and the weight of regret.
133 Marta Bevacqua/Trunk Archive
134 Sara Aït Benabdallah
137 Harry Gruyaert/Magnum Photos

ACKNOWLEDGEMENTS

I would like to extend my sincere thanks to Laura Paton and the team at Laurence King who helped bring this book to life. To the photographers featured in these pages: your approach to maximalist photography – your use of colour, density, texture and visual complexity – has been both inspiring and essential. Your work not only challenges how we usually see subjects in a photograph but also expands how we can tell stories in them.

To my daughter, Thea, thank you for your energy, your curiosity and the joyful chaos you bring into every day. You reminded me (often without knowing it) of the beauty in excess and the art in layering life fully. This book, in many ways, echoes your natural spirit.

To my mother, Shauneen and Estella, and to my father, who is deeply missed.

Finally, to you, the reader. Thank you for your continued engagement and willingness to see things differently. In a world that often values simplicity and speed, may this book encourage you to embrace complexity, find beauty in excess and discover the layered narratives hidden in every frame.